THE PART OF COUNSEL

Includes

THE BOOK OF WISDOM

Sister Thedra

Copyright © 2021 by Halls of Light, LLC

All rights reserved. This book or any portion thereof may not be reproduced or used in any manner whatsoever without the express written permission of the publisher except for the use of brief quotations in a book review.

ISBN: 978-1-7373071-3-6

To the Reader

Please read and review "Divine Explanations" on page 213 for questions and definitions of terms.

This book is only a portion of the teachings and prophecies that have been given by Sananda (Jesus Christ), Sanat Kumara, and others of the higher realms, and Recorded by Sister Thedra.

Contents

THE PART OF COUNSEL 1

THE PART OF WISDOM 53

BLESS THINE BROTHER 119

TRANSITION 171

Mission Statement 206

Sananda's Appearance 207

About the Late Sister Thedra 208

Divine Explanations 213

Other Books by TNT Publishing 224

Esu Jesus Sananda

This reproduction is from an actual photograph taken on June 1st, 1961, in Chichen Itza, Yucatan, by one of thirty archaeologists working in the area at the time. Sananda appeared in visible, tangible body and permitted His photograph to be taken.

THE PART OF COUNSEL

By the hand of One Sent shall ye receive the first part of a New Work and it shall begin this day - So let it be -- It shall be brot forth as the other which hast been done -- Ye shall bring forth this Work as nothing before - and it shall be for the Good of All that it is done - So let it be - Ye shall set aside a place wherein ye shall do the work - and wherein none shall distract thee - and ye shall be as one prepared - So be it and Selah -- Ye shall arise at an hour suitable and put thine house in order and come into the place which hast been set aside - and it shall be given unto thee -- So let it begin now - and it shall begin with this part herein and it shall be the first of the New Part ---

Say unto them in this manner - that the law shall be the law - yet the law of one realm holds good for that realm only - and likewise is the law changed from time to time - each people - each age -- And this is to be understood - that one law holds good for One people in One realm - yet others of other realms do not come under that law ---

While there are laws which hold good thruout ALL the inhabited Universes created and peopled - yet concern not thyself with these now for at this time thou needst but be concerned with thine own place and part - thine own orb - and part which ye play at this present time -- I say this is the day to be concerned with - this place/ plan/ and work at hand -- And it shall profit thee little to ask what the Earth rests on - while thine feet are sinking in quicksand ---

I say: Let it be understood that there are ones which have come from lands afar - which have been prepared to assist thee in this place wherein thou art - within the Earth/ the world of man -- And the foolishness of man is as nought unto them -- They hear not the foolish prayers of the selfish man - neither the cries of the unjust - for they too come under a law - by which they are allowed to enter into the world of man -- They come as ones prepared - and by the consent of the Mighty Council -- They bring with them naught - they come empty handed - and they ask nought -- They give of themself - and for this their reward shall be great - for theirs is a Selfless Mission -- Now I say unto thee: Be ye as one prepared to receive of these which come to assist thee -- They walk amongst thee as ones unsung - unknown and they ask only that ye be prepared to hear them out - and that ye be prepared for the Greater Part -- So be it - as ye are prepared so shall ye receive ---

Sori Sori -- I say unto thee: Ye shall give unto them which seek wisdom this part - and it shall profit them to accept it - for I have chosen this time and method to give it unto them -- This Mine Word shall be the Word of God - as set forth in Its purity -- Yet I say - thine language is insufficient to express the fullness of the perfection of The Word of God -- Neither can the beauty be captured by word or pen -- Neither hast there lived a man upon the Earth which hast Known the fullness of the Grandeur of Heaven - for he hast not experienced it - and until he hast experienced it he knows not ---

NOW I say: It is come when there shall be ones which know - shall visit thee - and they shall call thee by name and they shall tell thee of things which thou hast not seen - neither heard -- They shall be unto thee great Light - and direct thee in this part --They shall bring unto thee Great Knowledge and strength--

Now I say unto thee O Reader: Be ye not mistaken about this - for I am the Author and Finisher of Mine Work -- I have begun a Great Work and I shall finish it - and no man shall say Me "Nay!"---

While ye sleep I shall do. a work ye know not of -- Ye shall learn well thine lessons - then ye shall know wherein I have spoken - and ye shall remember well that which I have said ---

Blest are they which learn of Me and by Me -- So let thine mind be staid upon Me the Light - for I AM the LIGHT - out of the Light I come I am not limited to time or space -- I Am One with the ALL - known as Solen Aum Solen The Father ---

I Am Sent that this day bear fruit - and that the harvest be brot forth this day -- So let it suffice that I Am the One Sent that ye be awakened So be it I come that it be accomplished this day ---

While I speak unto thee in simple language that ye might comprehend - I say too that it is given in this manner for a reason which ye know not - therefore I beseech thee - criticize not the manner in which I give this Word - for it behooves thee to seek the meaning thereof - and hold thine tongue - for in thine criticism thou hast lost favor with Me -- In thine deceit and bigotry thou hast not found favor with Me ---

I say: Come unto me as a little child - put away thine conceit and thine puny ways - and I shall put within thine mouth Mine Words -- I shall touch thee and make of thee a prophet in thine own right ---

I have given unto this Mine Servant - the Authority and power to speak for Me - and I have lain Mine hand upon her head and pronounced the Word which hast prepared her to receive Me and of Me and she hast accounted for herself in the time of stress -- She hast remained true unto her trust - and she hast not betrayed herself or her trust -- I now give unto her this dictation - and she shall prepare it for them which seeks after such as she hast prepared for them -- And according to Mine command she shall not trespass upon anyone - neither shall she put words into thy mouth -- She shall do that which I ask of her - and she shall not trespass on thy free will. -- So be it I have sibored her for this day - and the days which are yet to come ---

Behold ye the work of the Lord -- Behold ye the hand of God - see it move - for it shall move the length and breadth of the Earth -- It shall move before it ALL which shall oppose it - the Light -- It shall bring into the Light all that is of the Light - and that which is not of the Light shall be no more seen of man - for it shall return unto its nothingness.

I Am Come that I might set men aright - set them upright - upon their feet - that they might bear their own weight - and be responsible for their own deeds and for themself -- Each shall study well himself - his deeds and the responsibility thereof ---

I come that he be made responsible -- So be it that I Am He which is sent at this time for this part - and I shall not stop Mine Work until I am finished! ---

Think ye O man - that I am a puny priest - one of failure and exile? Neither have I forsaken Mine part - Mine Office - for I have been ordained of Mine Father for this part which I shall finish with honor and dignity ---

I shall triumph over evil - and put to shame the evil doer - the slanderer and the whoremonger - the hypocrites and blasphemers -- For

I shall do a wondrous Work - and they shall stand ashamed before Me for they shall see themself as they are -- I say unto thee O man of Earth: Cleanse thineself of all deceit - hypocrisy and bigotry - and prepare thineself for the days ahead - for ye shall continue thine days after thou hast put aside thine mortal flesh -- Be ye not deceived in this - think not to escape the law -- Enter into no unholy alliance with the forces of darkness - for I tell thee of a surety - they would deceive thee -- For it is the law: "As ye are prepared so shall ye receive" -- Give unto this much thot - ponder well Mine Word - and be ye mindful of Mine Sayings - for it shall profit thee much ---

Now I come as a thief in the night - I find thee off guard - thou hast been babbling and mumbling the sayings of the ancients - of times long past -- Yet I ask of thee: think ye were one of them? - think ye were there? - then why mumble - then why turn unto these ancient words - when I place before thee the present day - that which shall feed thee and satisfy thine longings - and fill thine needs -- I bring unto thee this day a part designed to fill thine needs - and to prepare thee for the days ahead ---

It is now come when man shall stand shorn of all self-glory - of all his pomp and ceremony - and he shall stand as naked before the Great and Mighty Tribunal -- He shall have nothing with which to cover his shame -- He shall be as one exposed unto the Light wherein all things are revealed ---

So be it I say: Cleanse out all the impure thots - all the impure -- And beat not thine breast in supplication to any ancient priest or lord - For I say unto thee: Cleanse thine own temple - and I shall enter in and abide with thee -- Put no name above The Name of Solen Aum Solen - The One Which hast given unto thee Being -- Let no man say unto thee there is One higher -- Yet I say: He Solen Aum Solen IS - hast always been - yet He hast been called many Names in many tongues - and the Name matters not - for this day I speak unto thee of THIS DAY -- And ye which speak the language in which I am speaking shall be set apart for a Work which shall be different from all other -- Ye shall be designated by a number and a color - and ye shall stand - stand upon the Precepts of The Mighty and Holy Council which hast brot forth a Mighty Country ---

I say: Ye shall stand upon the Precepts and Concepts which hast been set forth in the founding of thy Mighty Nation -- Ye shall stand as a people apart from all others ---

Yet ye shall not adorn thyself in fine raiment - and boast of thine success - while thy Brothers crawl on their bellies before thee begging bread ---

I say: Ye shall stand apart as a living example of the Light which I AM -- Ye shall not be as the idolaters - ye shall worship only The Source of thy being - and ye shall not give unto any man the power to forgive thee thine transgressions - neither shall any man give unto thee passport into the Heavenly Kingdoms ---

It is said: "Ye shall have no false gods - NO GOD before ME" - So be it that I say unto thee: Have NONE save The Father of ALL - The O - Solen Aum Solen - for thou art ensouled in Him -- In Him thou hast thine BEing and there is naught save HIM ---

Bring unto Him thineself in Holy Reverence - and ask of Him forgiveness - and cleanse out the unseen places wherein thou hast hidden thine inmost thots and deeds -- Know ye - nothing is hidden from Him - for He is THE ALL SEEING EYE ---

Be ye as a little child - hold out thy hand in humble submission unto His Will - and He shall give unto thee according unto thy preparation.

Sori Sori -- Let this be unto them Mine Testimony - that they might know from whence cometh the Authority for this part - and for this Word -- I say unto thee:

I have given unto thee power and the authority to speak in Mine Name - and thou hast not put thine hand into their pockets - neither have they troubled themself to assist thee -- Yet I say: I shall bring forth One which shall give unto thee the assistance which is needful - and he shall find his reward great - for I say - there is such unknown wealth stored up for him as he hast not seen -- Yet he shall ask no reward on Earth nor in heaven - for he shall serve for the joy of serving -- So be it that he shall ask no other reward ---

Now ye shall bring forth a New Part - and this one shall be called "The Part of Counsel"- the part which is for the Counselors -- The Council shall direct and put forth such Work as is needful at this time - and when there is a need it shall be filled - this I declare unto thee ---

Before there is another moon - ye shall see many changes - and many new things shall be shown unto thee -- While it is not yet time to reveal all which shall be shown unto thee - ye shall wait for the time and place -- I have said I shall bring thee into a place and show thee many new things - and it is so -- So be it ye shall abide with Me and wait upon Me - and I shall deal justly with thee ---

While I say I shall deal justly with thee - I say: As ye give so shall ye receive -- So be it that I give unto thee of Mineself - So shall it be with thee - and they which receive of thee shall be unto thee mindful of Me - for as I have given unto thee and thou hast given unto them - so do they receive of Me - thru thee -- Therefore it is required of them to be mindful of thee - for art thou not Mine Servant - and is a Servant not the representation of his Master's House - and is he not worthy of recognition? So be it that I send thee forth as Mine Messenger - as Mine hand and foot made manifest unto them ---

I have Ordained thee Mine Priestess - and Mine Priestess shall be honored for the Service rendered unto mankind in Mine Name -- So be it I have spoken and thou hast heard Me - and thou hast recorded it as I have spoken -- So be it this shall be made available unto them which hunger for Light - for I say unto them: I have set One apart and Ordained that One as Mine Priestess - and it behooves thee to know and to heed that which I say unto thee - thru and by this means - and by her hand shall the Word of God go forth as it is spoken --

Even as it is spoken shall it go forth - without embellishment or change of any kind for by this method shall I know the true from the false for I have said unto thee:- Change not the WORD OF GOD - for it shall stand on its own merits ---

I am now prepared to speak of thine own world - of preparation and many things concerning thee and that which ye know not of ---

Let it be said - that there are ones now within thine midst - which are prepared to give unto thee the Cup of Living Water ---

And they shall be as Mine hands and as Mine feet -- They shall be fleet of foot and quick of Spirit - for Mine Spirit shall abide in them and they shall Know themself to be One with Me ---

They shall commune with Me - and they shall not be deceived - for they shall Know Me for that which I am - The Lord of Lords - The Host of Hosts - and I Am He Which is Sent that a mighty Work be done -- So shall it be according to The Father's Will ---

Before We proceed with this Work - let it be understood that there are ones which deny Me - Mine existence - Mine Word - Mine Servants Yet I say: They but betray themself - they are want to know Me - and they but deny The Father Which hast Sent Me -- For as they deny Me so do they deny The Father Solen Aum Solen - THE SOURCE OF THEIR BEING -- And as they deny Mine Servant - Mine Word - so do they deny Me –

I am come that they might KNOW! Yet they fear - they fear for themself - for their fortunes - for their children!

Yet when I reach out Mine hand unto them that they be lifted up - I hear them say: It is an impossible situation - it is an incurable disease it is an absolute thing which no man can correct - no man can change - and they call Me an imposter ---

Poor - impoverished are they - for they have been under the yoke for long - and they are yet bound unto the old order - might I say - the old "order of thinkers" yea - they think themselves to be thus and so - while they go about as robots -- They think not in their own right - they have no thots of their own - for all inspiration comes from Spirit -

whether it be for weal or woe -- None are without guidance - be it high or low - I say: None are without guidance!! ---

While I say - each unto his own preparation shall he receive - (for it is the law) ---

Now I speak unto them which are prepared to receive this Mine Word - and none shall deny it ---

There is a place prepared for each and every Being which exists - even in all worlds -- There is a time allotted unto each and every one - There is a plan which is given unto each one as he comes into physicality - and he knows the part which he is to play - yet there are many - too many - which forget - these I am speaking to now ---

I say: Arise ye which sleepeth!

Arise ye which are dead!

Arise ye which hear Mine Voice and I shall touch thee - I shall quicken thee and ye shall KNOW even as I Know ---

I say: Follow ye Me - for I have gone before thee - I Know the way. It is for this that I bid thee <u>follow</u> Me - for I have gone the long way to find thee -- I have called unto thee thru the centuries - I have searched thee out - I have stood thee upright on thine feet and thou hast fallen asleep again - yea - even on thine feet thou hast slept! Thou hast fallen asleep even in Mine embrace ---

Now I say: Thou hast slept overtime - now ye shall awaken and come forth as ones alive - as ones willing to stay awake ---

Think ye not that I shall always abide with thee - for I shall take Mine leave of thee - even as I come -- Is it not said that "I shall come as a thief in the night" - wast it not done - wast it not so? ---

I came! Didst thou know the day - the hour? I say unto thee: Thou knew not the hour! Neither shall ye know the hour of Mine departure.

Now - fain would I speak unto thee of thine frailties - thine weakness - for thou knowest them - thou seest them -- Yet ye shall not point thine finger at thine fellow men - for are they worse - or better than thou - wherein hast thou attained perfection? Call not thine brother foolish - so long as thou thinkest thine ownself to be wise - for I say: Ye know not the freedom of the Universe - ye know not the freedom of man ---

Thou art bound - even in thine thinking! I say ye know not how nor what to think - for thou art a confused people - a confused people - I say!! ---

I come that ye might KNOW - that ye might learn of Me - the Law of the Universe - the law which makes all men one ---

I am the Lawgiver for this day -- I come not to set aside the old law yet to reveal unto thee greater Law -- For it is now come when man shall expand his world - and he shall pass beyond his boundaries - as ones free from the gravitation of the Earth and the attraction of the Moon ---

So be it I am well prepared for Mine part - for long have I been traversing the Universe - yea - the Universes without number do I know as the palm of Mine hand I know them ---

So be it I say unto thee: Arise! and come unto Me and I shall show unto thee greater glories than thou hast dreamed of -- So be it I am He which guards the portal - and I shall guard well the Portal - for all within is Mine -- All that is without is as nothing to Me ---

I say: All that is within is Mine - for I am the Keeper of Mine Father's fortune -- All that He has He hast endowed unto Me - I shall not be tray Mine trust ---

I speak unto thee of the Universes without number - I Know the number thereof -- Knowest thou the number of the stars in the heavens?

I say unto thee: Thou knowest not the Stars in thy heavens - yet there are more Universes than stars visible unto thy sight ---

I say unto thee: BEHOLD THE GLORY OF THE HEAVENS! And be ye as one blest -- Behold the Handiwork of thy God Which created the Earth and the Heavens thereof!!---

Sori Sori -- Mine hand I place upon thine head - and I speak the Word which shall be unto thee the Authority to speak in Mine Name - and to use Mine Name - and for the Good of ALL mankind shall it be .Now ye shall place thine hand in Mine - and I shall direct thee into the place wherein ye shall be given yet greater power -- And by the Grace of Mine Father shall it be done unto thee even as it is done unto Me ---

So be it that there stands by a Mighty Host to assist in the Work at hand - and it shall be done -- No man shall say unto Us nay - for we shall stand as Sentinels over them which have volunteered to serve life in the physical flesh -- I say - they serve not alone - for flesh is weak indeed - and it is for Us of the Host that they receive their strength and direction ---

I say it is from the Host which stands by - that they receive their strength and direction -- We direct their activities - and give unto them strength to carry out their activity which they have chosen - even before taking embodiment in flesh ---

While I say there are ones which stand by as Sentinels - I too say that They neither force nor coerce - They neither persuade nor hinder - They wait for the one who would serve - to offer up himself in Holy surrender - as the living sacrifice - that all mankind might be blest ---

There are ones who say: "Help me" - yet wherein have they given that they <u>be</u> helped?

Wherein have they helped?

I say: It is within every man's capacity to do something to lift up his fellow man - yet he does nothing that lifts him - while he puts his hand into the pocket of another and asks alms from them ---

There are ones which give of his Earthly substance while he does it grudgingly -- He finds no reward in this for it shall return unto him as a burning and flaming sword ---

There are ones which administer unto the sick grudgingly - yet they find they are not comforted - neither shall they find comfort ---

For they have not given of themself - therefore the gift is not considered valid - for without the giver the gift is invalid in the sight of The Father ---

So be it there are ones which give for the self-gratification - to be seen of men - to receive of them praise and esteem -- These have already received their reward - for none other shall they find - none other!

There are ones which give of themself - and this is the gift which is acceptable unto the Lord of Lords - the King of Kings - The Father Solen Aum Solen -- So be it the only gift which He can accept -- Therein is the Secret of man's greatest joy ---

Blest is the giver when the gift is bestowed with love and joy - and with the joy which is of the heart ---

Blest is the one which gives of his substance - yet greater is the Gift of <u>Selfless</u> <u>Service</u> - for this is the accredited gift in our sight ---

Blest is he which receives such gifts given in selfless service - for they are the recipients of Love-- That is the love of which I speak - the Selfless Love -- Yet there are ones which know not the meaning of Love -- Unto these I say: Go into the stables and watch the mother with her lamb - the mother with her foal - the mother with her calf and see if thine love is any greater - any higher - any <u>greater</u> I say ---

When thou canst love with the greater love - thou hast risen out of the stable!

I say unto thee: Arise and be ye as a fit vessel to serve Me in Mine place of abode ---

Be ye as one brot forth this day on the wings of Love -- Be ye as one acceptable unto The Lord of Hosts - and be ye as one called out - and ye shall be given a place upon the right hand of God The Father - and He shall bless thee and ye shall be glad ---

Many are called - few are chosen - why? They have not kept their covenant - they have betrayed themself -- These shall sorrow mightily for they shall be cast aside to wait in darkness - they shall know not the joy of the one which sits upon The Father's right hand ---

There are ones which go forth preaching strange and false doctrines. These are as the fools prattling the sayings of the ancients or moderns -- These are as the ones which are led about by some unknown, untried Spirit which makes mockery of the "Spirit" - and they are in no wise learned of the LAW - the GREATER LAW - the Law under which they live and have their being ---

They are to be pitied - for they know not that they do not know - they think themself wise -- Yet I say poor in Spirit are they - for they are as ones under a 'spell' - they are deluded from the first ---

Wherein is it said: "That there are ones which would lead thee astray and hold thee captive" -- It is so - yet it is said: I come that ye be led out of captivity - I come that ye be delivered out of bondage ---

Therefore it behooves thee to seek the Light and I shall hear thine supplications - and consider them -- Let it be said that I am mindful of all thine goings - thine comings - and all thine deeds -- Every thot I know and I have said: Purify thineself - put aside thine foolishness - ask of The Father forgiveness for all thine shortcomings - and one shall come unto thee and give unto thee as thou art prepared to receive - so shall it be ---

Let it be known that there are ones which have betrayed themself many times - they have given of themself that the evil one be served --

They have forgotten that which hast been given unto them to do - that which they came to do ---

These are the ones which are now groping in darkness - they have the will to serve the Light - yet they know not which way to go -- They cry out for help - knowing not from whence it cometh - and fearing their prayers are not heard -- Yet unto them is given a part - the part of preparation ---

They again are entrusted with the WORD - and they have but to accept it -- While they have a fear of being deceived - they fear! They fear! - and they turn unto their friends asking solace -- Wherein have they been comforted? Now I ask: Wherein have they found solace or comfort ---

Blest is he which takes comfort of Me - for I shall touch him and he shall come to know Mine touch ---

I come that these be awakened - that they might be brot out of their bondage - that they might come to know as I know ---

Wherefore I bring with Me a Host of helpers from the realms of Light -- A band of Angelic helpers which have for a great part clothed themself in mortal flesh - that this day might be the fulfilling of a great and mighty plan ---

Therefore - I am come not alone. While thou hast slept a great Work hast been done - yet it is not finished - and thou hast not seen the finish thereof -- It shall come to pass that man of this present generation shall arise as on the beams of light - and he shall soar unto heights yet unknown unto him -- Yet I say unto thee - O man: Be ye the unknowing one - be ye not puffed up in thy conceit - thine unknowing - for there aware of his Guard - his Directors -- His willfulness hast separated him from Them ---

He hast <u>thot</u> himself separate - free - and a thing apart - while he hast been as one Earth bound ---

He hast been as a castout - as an exile - a wayward Son - while The Father calls unto him to return unto his abiding place ---

He gives for the most part little heed unto the call -- For the most part he hast his fingers in his ears - that he might not hear ---

When it is come that he suffers greatly - he cries out for relief - and strength -- Yet when he is healed he goes his way in his forgetfulness - paying no heed unto them which hast been unto his succor ---

There are ones which suffer for the sake of mankind -- These are ones that have taken up the flesh garments that they do a work which shall profit their fellowmen ---

These ask no reward save that they serve life in its full -- I say: They ask naught of any man -- They sacrifice self in selfless service -- They are the ones which walk in silence and strut not before man - to be seen and heard of man - that they gain favor of him -- They walk humbly and safely amongst the bigots and hypocrites - the infidels and the idol worshipers ---

They fear no man - neither the tongue nor the foot do they fear ---

Yet it is said that the tongue of the asp stingeth not like the tongue of man -- Too - it is said that: woe unto anyone whichsoever that sets foot against one of Mine Servants -- They fear not - for they know Mine hand is upon them ---

They ask not freedom from pain that they escape the suffering -- They ask not favors of Me The Lord God-- They ask not for recognition of men - -- they are as ones which know wherein they are staid -- They are satisfied to follow where I lead them -- They fret not for small things They are comforted that I am their Counselor - that I am with them - and they know Mine Voice and respond unto it ---

Sori Sori -- There is a plan - a great and noble plan for man - and it behooves thee to know the part which thou hast chosen - I say unto thee thou hast chosen a noble part ---

Yet it is not an easy one - for the part thou hast chosen hast not been one of great favor with man-- It is the part for which I have prepared thee -- I have called thee forth as a Servant of the Great and Mighty God of Creation -- I have ordained thee as the Son of God -- I have given unto thee passport into Mine place of abode - and no man shall deny thee entrance -- I say: PASS - pass ye shall -- Place thine hand in Mine and I shall lead thee every step of the way - for this have I called thee forth -- I Know thee and thine every thot-- I have watched thee - and I shall not forsake thee - neither shall Mine Word become invalid.

When it is come that man has made his final play within the flesh - he shall stand as one attired in yet another body - yet it shall be unlike the flesh -- While he shall have the same pattern - he shall not have the atomic - heavy body of Earth's Substance - he shall have a body which shall be of Light Substance - of the <u>Substance</u> of <u>Light</u> -- He shall wear it as a garment not not unlike the one he hast worn - yet it shall not be unto him a bond - a bound -- He shall have many bodies in his ascent -

for he shall go from glory unto glory - each shall be more Glorious - more beautiful - lighter - and at last he shall be free of all fetters - all bounds - ALL FETTERS - for AT LAST he shall be as I AM ---

Sori Sori -- I am come that man be lifted up -- There is but little time allotted unto him for his time - within the Earth is but short -- And at no time have I given unto him the Word which is designed to frighten him - rather would I awaken him from his sleep ---

He is asleep -- Some in deep sleep - others have begun to stir - while others are awake ---

I say: For the most part man sleepeth yet ---

Now it is come when certain ones shall go out from the Inner Temple - which shall do a great and Mighty Work among men of Earth.

They shall take up mortal flesh and walk among men as man -- They shall come under the law of flesh -- While <u>others</u> shall come as ones in flesh - which shall not come under the law of Earth - these shall appear as man - these shall do the work of man with the tools of man - Yet they shall supersede all man's achievements - for they shall have such knowledge that has as yet not been revealed unto man -- They shall be as the <u>revelators</u> - they shall bring with them such knowledge as man hast not yet dreamed -- They shall prepare the way for yet others which are to follow them -- For this do many wait - that they come into the Earth - that they might be part of the new Earth - the establishing of "The New Earth" - and they are well qualified ---

For they have been well schooled - they have been prepared in many a school which man of Earth hast not known ---

It is said that many come from afar to study man and Earth - that they might be prepared to assist in her restoration ---

I say unto thee O man of Earth: Thou art a curiosity unto others far afield -- Thou art as ones groping in darkness -- Thou as yet are not aware of thine own inheritance - yet ye boast in thine absolute ignorance-- I say: Thou art ignorant of the many schools wherein thine brothers labor that ye be helped - that ye be assisted at this time ---

Ye know not the number of Ambassadors and Messengers which have given of themself - that hast lowered their Light to come into the Earth that man be enlightened ---

Yet man in his ignorance hast profaned and defamed the Name of the One which hast been so Merciful unto the wayward and unknowing ones as thou art ---

I say: "Unknowing" for thou hast fallen from thine high estate - thou hast fallen lower than the beast -- For it is given unto the beast to be dumb - yet unto thee hast been given the gift of speech - and thou hast adulterated it - thou hast blasphemed the <u>Word</u> - the <u>Name</u> of thine Father which hast given unto thee Being ---

I say: Thou art slothful and afrighted - for thou hast "sinned" before HIM ---

Thou hast fared far worse than the beast - for the beast knows no repentance - and it is given unto man to have the knowledge of right and wrong - for to know puts him in the class of man -- Yet he repents not - he places himself in jeopardy - and his inheritance awaits him - or he repents and claims it -- Then he returns no more unto his filthy ways unto his old ways -- He goes forth as one sober and alert - as one aware of his Source - as one alive and he gives credence unto his Source -- He walks humbly - upright as a Son of God -- He bows before no false gods -- He worships no idols and he fortunes unto himself that which The Father Wills for him ---

There is a time and a place set aside for each and every one - each unto his own preparation -- Each shall be in his own environment - as he hast prepared himself -- There is no cast which shall hold him - yet he shall be as one which shall find himself in <u>his</u> <u>place</u> - and that shall be as he hast prepared for himself ---

For it is said: Prepare thyself for the Greater Part -- Yet I ask of thee: What hast thou done? What hast thou done? Hast thou repented - hast thou turned thine face homeward - hast thou loved thine neighbor as thine own self? Hast thou given of thineself that others be comforted? Hast thou given succor unto the comfortless - unto the sick and dying? OR - hast thou sat in the seat of the bigot - and appraised thine own worthiness - greater than thine fellow man -- Hast thou denied him comfort while thou hast wasted thy substance -- Hast thou laughed at his foolishness while thou hast called thyself "Wise" ---

Now I ask of thee: Hast thou been worthy to judge thy fellowman? Hast thou been so wise as to judge righteous judgment -- Hast thou been so wise as to give unto him of thine own substance? Hast thou been so wise as to put aside thy foolishness? Hast thou been as one blameless - without blemish ---

I ask of thee: Hast thou turned from thy childish ways - art thou as one without "Sin"? ---

Ponder well these Mine Words! And answer not ere thou hast thot well upon them!

Blameless ye shall stand before the throne of The Most High Living God ere thou canst answer: "Yea Lord - I am blameless!" ---

So be it there are none which deceiveth Him - He is as The ALL - One with All - and in Him All are One -- He is not a "Thing" - yet He is ALL that is Real - All that is Eternal ---

Deceive not thyself O man - there is a Plan - a time - a place - and the time is come when ye shall bestir thyself - and come forth as one prepared -- Now I say: Ye shall come forth -- What is thine preparation? What thine qualifications? ---

Wherein hast thou prepared thyself for to receive thine Sonship - art thou so qualified? ---

Wherein hast thou been faithful in all things? Wherein hast thou served the Lord thy God with thine whole heart - all thine strength - all thy might? ---

Wherein hast thou given thyself in Holy Sacrifice? With all thine heart - all thineself - thou shall serve Him -- And know ye this: He hast called unto thee from out the Inner Temple - yet hast thou said: "Here I Am Lord - SEND ME!" ---

Send Me? I say yea thou! I am saying: COME! Come All ye that have a mind - the will to serve Me - for Mine is the Greater Part ---

I say: "MINE is the GREATER PART" - and unto <u>thee</u> I say: Come! and I shall touch thee - and no man shall call ME a liar - for I say unto <u>thee</u>: PROVE ME! ---

Let it be understood that I am not amongst the spirits of the "dead". I am the Risen Lord -- I am The One Sent of Mine Father that HIS WILL be made manifest among - and in man upon the Earth this day.

Behold ME - for I stand a living testimony of Mine Father's Will - for I Am His Will - none other do I have ---

I come that ye might be found and unbound -- By All the Love which is Mine I come - by the consent of the Great and Mighty Council I come - for thou art in dire need - and thou hast not known how dire thine need---

I say: Thou art in dire need! So be it I Know! I see - I Come - I act according unto the law -- I Know the law - and I am come that it be fulfilled - So let it be -- Aforehand I have informed thee of a Mighty Work - and ye shall see and know -- As thou art prepared so shall ye be given -- Ye shall increase thy capacity for understanding and love - and with all thy knowledge get understanding ---

Sori Sori -- This is the time of great stress for the peoples of the Earth - and We of the Council are concerned with the welfare of the people -- Wherefore We come that there be great learning - and that peace might be established in the Earth ---

Yet We labor long and without favor - without recognition - without glory amongst them ---

They present themself as a pawn before us - a pawn to be won - and we weary not of our work for we come with the consent of Our Council that this Work <u>be</u> <u>done</u> - and we ask not glory or recognition as man of Earth asks---

We will that they be lifted up - that they receive of us that which we have for them -- When this is done then we shall make known unto them that which hast been concealed from them - then we shall show our hand - and work with them as brothers ---

Be ye informed that there is no desire on our part to withhold anything - yet I say: They are as yet not prepared to learn that which we know -- We have long been in the Schools of Great learning - outside of thy own Galaxy -- Thine own Galaxy is but a small part of our learning - for we go from galaxy unto galaxy with ease - while thou art unable to traverse thine small sector of the Earth --

With great ease we go from planet unto planet - with greater ease than ye go from nation to nation - for thou art a divided people -- We need no passports - no great "red tape" - for we are known - and we know -- There is no confusion amongst us of the realms known unto us - of which we belong ---

There are the ones which do not deal with such as the Earth and her people - while there are ones which do -- These have volunteered - these are prepared and they know where to find the ones which are to be brot out -- I say: These are aware of them which are to be brot out.

There is no secrets unto them - for long have they been watching - and waiting the time when they might step forth and assist in this work.

The hour hast now struck when great changes shall take place - there shall be GREAT CHANGES! - And shall be the ones which shall change - for he shall first change - then other changes for good shall follow ---

Many have heard the Word - many have seen the Vision - many have given of themself that this be done ---

Now it is come when the ones which are of a mind to follow the counsel of The Council - shall learn that which hast been prepared for them - for there are provisions made for each and every one so prepared. I say: "As ye are prepared so shall ye receive" ---

Now the ones which are sent sit in Council daily - yea hourly - for the sole purpose of counseling thee -- They are not asleep or in lethargy they watch and wait ---

Be ye as one prepared to receive them -- It is given unto them to work in many ways - MANY WAYS - unknown unto thee - yet they trespass not upon thy free will -- They coerce not - they boast not - they are an humble assembly -- They fear not - neither do they ask alms of any man ---

Let it be understood that there are ones which abide in the Earth as man - which are not of the Earth - neither are they of the nether worlds.

I say: There are ones which have come into thine world as ones of another order of beings -- They take up flesh as the <u>Sacrificial Robe</u> - they come that man might be lifted up - they come as one of flesh - yet they are not born of woman ---

Wherein is it said - that there are ones which are of another order which walk as man ---

When it is understood that which is said unto thee thou shall comprehend many things which now confound and confuse thee ---

There <u>are</u> <u>ones</u> from the nether world - there are ones which come from the dark regions - yet these come thru the womb of woman ---

Another order comes by other means which ye know not - these are intruders! INTRUDERS!! ---

I speak of them that ye might know that all which come are not of the Light -- Fain would I speak of <u>these</u> - yet it is well that ye know the true from the false -- Close not thine ear unto Me - for I would have ye know <u>All</u> things which should prepare thee for the days ahead ---

I say unto thee - it is thine own salvation that ye be prepared - So let it be ---

Be ye not unmindful of The Mighty Source -- Be ye not forgetful of thy part - and be ye as ones mindful of all thine blessings ---

Wherein hast thy judgment been of greater importance than now? Ye shall at <u>all</u> times be as one informed - and ye shall be as one prepared to judge before making hasty judgment ---

Yet I shall give unto thee discernment - and comprehension - in all these matters ---

Too - I say: Deceive not thineself - for it is given unto men to be dreamers - they imagine <u>great</u> and vain imaginings - and <u>they</u> <u>are</u> <u>not</u> learned ---

They are prone to speak hastily in their vain imagings -- Their vanity prompts them to speak of things they know not of ---

For this hast he been as a foolish child prattling his sayings -- Therein is the vanity of man - he is want to be heard and seen ---

Be ye as one which KNOWS whereof ye speak -- Be ye <u>in</u>lightened and ye shall profit therefrom/ therein---

Blest is he which knows that which he says to be of the Light --

Blest is he which hast controlled his tongue --

Blest is he which knows the power of speech --

Blest is he which uses that power to glorify The Father which hast given unto him speech --

Blest is he which KNOWS the Wisdom of Silence ---

By the hand of the Mighty Council hast the children of Earth been cared for - and by the Mercy of Our Father has it been so -- For the children of Earth hast been a wayward lot -- They have gone into darkness of their own account - and they have turned away from the Light - they have denied the Source of their being ---

There are ones which have followed after them - which are lost in darkness - that they be reminded of their Source - that they be brot out of their darkness - their bondage -- I am come as one of them -- Sent of Mine Father Am I ---

Now I bring with Me a host which are of the mind to assist them - even unto the end -- Yet many of these are not of flesh - ne're have they been - ne're shall they be - for it is given unto them to be of another order ---

Another Order I say -- These are of another time - another place - and they are the Guardians of Greater realms - greater peoples -- They are well aware of the plight of this people of Earth -- They are well aware of the conditions in which they move and have their being (the people of Earth) - they too - know by what Authority they are sent forth. They ask no man aught - for they are self-sufficient - they are reliable for they have long been prepared for this day ---

Yet man knows not the ones which are fortuned such knowledge -- They are want to think themself self-sufficient while it is <u>not so</u> -- They are prone to flattery and bigotry - while they are bound in darkness and bondage ---

Now it is come when they shall cry out for the assistance of these which are Sent ---

By their assistance shall the people of the Earth be delivered out - for it is now come when the Earth hast entered into a new place upon her long journey into the unknown place of space - and time -- There is great danger - for I say the Earth is the proving ground - the Laboratory and the insane asylum of the Universe -- It is the place set aside as the testing ground - the School of the probationers - and for this is it called the lowest in the system ---

I say - it is the School for Gods - for none less could do that which is to be done -- There is a <u>great</u> Service to be rendered here - now - and for this do We of The Great and Mighty come forth as ones to assist.

For the Earth is a much beloved and Great entity - which We shall bring thru her time of travail -- And it behooves each and every child of Earth to know their part -- It is a crucial time - a time of birth - a time of testing - weighing and sorting ---

This is the time long foretold - when it would appear great and mysterious "things" in the skies - and the heavens shall give up their secrets -- So be it - unto them which are worthy to receive - they shall be revealed ---

I am speaking now for the Good of All men everywhere - yet I know wherein they are which are prepared for this day - for a greater work - for another place - another great revelation -- I am not so foolish as to reveal the unknown mysteries unto the unprepared - the ones which would betray their trust and themself ---

I place before them a plan - and they shall see but part - for no man seeth in toto - the completeness of such plans of which I speak - for they comprehend not the whole - for the whole concerns many a world,- many a people - many systems of worlds - people of greater orders than the Earthians ---

Lo - it is come when the sabers shall rattle in thy closets - and the hearth stones shall be cold - and the wheat shall be no more -- The land shall be desolate and the mother shall weep for her unborn -- So be it she shall wail loud and sorely for her unborn! She shall ask deliverance for her children's children - and she shall perish with them ---

Sori Sori -- Say unto them. They shall fear the law -- They shall account for themself - for their deeds -- They shall bring up their children to be accountable for <u>themself</u> - they shall bring them up in the way of righteousness - and forget not that I am come that they be made responsible!

I say unto them: For this did I come - for this I Am come - for this do I give unto thee the law -- It is exact and each and every mortal comes under the law which I give unto them ---

When one comes into the Earth - takes upon themself garments of flesh, he hast made a covenant with ME - and he comes for a purpose, for the purpose is he allowed to enter into the world of form - yet he forgets the purpose - therein is the pity!

He goes in and out of flesh as the unknowing one - he forgets from whence he came - neither whither he goeth - yet he hast been told aforehand - he hast read his records aforehand -- He hast two ways to go - and wherein hast he found his way back - for that matter he is lost, he hast become confused and bewildered - he hast followed many strange gods ---

Now I come - even as of <u>Old</u> declaring this is the <u>new day</u> - the time of the end - ye shall hear me this day! For I am not to be put aside - I am not to be mocked - neither am I to be put aside or cast out!

I say it is the time and the place to be about Mine Father's business for this hast He sent me - for this am I speaking into thee ---

Ye shall remember well that which I say - for it is most personal - I speak unto thee O reader - I speak unto each and every one which hast a mind - an ear - and I bid thee come forth this day and prepare thineself

For it cometh soon when ye shall go forth into a strange land - and ye shall find therein that which shall be strange unto thee - it shall be new and it behooves me to tell thee that there is no death -- Ye shall find that ye shall step from thine worn garment into another more befitting And is it not said many times: "As ye are prepared so shall ye receive". It is the law ---

Weary not of mine sayings - yet ye have not comprehended them - Listen unto me - give ear and I shall give unto thee comprehension - for there is a part for thee - and for this ye shall be prepared ---

I am he which knows wherein thou art bound - and I am come that ye be unbound -- Yet thou hast first to do that which is required of thee and it is clearly stated that ye shall walk in the way of the Lord -- Ye shall comply with the law which I give unto thee - and <u>then</u> I shall do my part ---

Be ye as one prepared - for at no time shall ye enter into the Holy of Holies unprepared -- Thy past glories shall be of no account - thine vain glory shall be of no account - for all thy vanity shall be as the legiron which shall bind thee ---

I say - put aside all thine pride - all thine pettiness - all thine hatred/ intolerance/ all thine <u>foolishness</u> - and be ye alert and watchful -- Hear ye me - and I shall speak unto thee of things profitable unto thee ---

Forget not that I am he which is Sent -- I come as The Father's will made manifest in me ---

I come as thy benefactor - as thy Counselor - as the forerunner of that which ye shall become -- I say: follow ye me and I shall lead thee out of bondage ---

Fear not! follow ye me - I shall deal justly with thee - and no man shall call me a fraud - and imposter - for I shall prove mineself ---

Be ye aware of them which hold out their hand asking alms of thee that they receive their reward for "the <u>Word</u>"- for no price is put on <u>Mine</u> <u>Word</u> -- I say I give freely - I ask nought of thee - save obedience unto the law - therefore I say unto thee: Ye shall first receive Mine Servants - even as ye would receive me - then I shall honor thee - for thou hast in like manner received me <u>and</u> mine servant -- Honor first mine servant - then I shall remember thee ---

Sori Sori -- By the hand of the Great and Divine Council shall ye be given this part of Counsel -- It shall be for the good of all - yet there are ones which shall refuse it - unto them is given the lesser part -- Unto them which receive it is given the Greater part ---

When they have rejected it they shall be as the ones left unto the lesser parts - they shall wait for the Greater ---

Now ye shall send forth this part as that which hast been given unto thee -- Ask of them no penny - and be ye as one prepared for the next part -- There shall be a next part - and it too shall go unto them in the same manner -- For this is it given unto thee in parts - they shall ponder well each part - and remember well that which is said herein in these parts ---

It is given unto me to observe them - and to know that which they do with it -- Therefore I say unto them: Be ye thotful of me and of mine counsel ---

I am apt at this - and I for that matter - have been at this for a long while - therefore I know what I am about ---

For this time I give unto thee these letters - and they shall be as personal letters unto YE the Reader -- Each shall receive it in his own way - and interpret it in his own tongue -- None shall place his own interpretation upon it <u>for</u> <u>another</u> -- Each shall find herein hidden that which another may <u>not</u> find - for I shall do a strange thing - I shall hide up Mine Word from the unjust and the imprudent - while I shall show the just and humble that which is hidden from the un just -- Therefore I say: Watch ye with diligence - read ye with eyes that see - and be ye alert unto that which ye see---

It is now come when I shall seek out the ones which are prepared to go all the way with me -- I am come that they be found and gathered in - blest shall they be ---

Now think ye not that I am not a person - for hast not Mine Father Given unto ME personality - think ye that I am a figment of man's mind, hast his mind deluded him in this? ---

I am as the Eternal Son of God -- Bear ye in mind I am Sent of Him the SOURCE of thy BEING - that ye might know thine eternal Source and Self ---

For that is the <u>real</u> - the eternal - while flesh is but the mortal garment - temporary at best - fleeting - and it perishes even as all mortal material - for it goes back into the Substance from whence it came ---

I speak unto thee of the duality - the two-fold personality -- There is the two-fold - ye know the one of flesh - yet ye but dream of the other which is as a "hope" as a dream -- Yet I say unto thee: Ye are not flesh, flesh but hides thine innermost Self - thine true identity ---

Think ye not that I know ye by flesh -- I know thine true identity - for I see that which ye know not - that which is forever thine mark - thine very Self - which is the same yesterday and forever - this is the Light which <u>never</u> fails ---

I come that it might not be hidden within the flesh -- It is said: "Let thine Light shine forth that all might see it"- it is for this that I come - that ye - the sleeper might awake and come forth and KNOW thineself to be alive -- Fashion for thyself no legiron - bring thineself unto me as a little child - as a living sacrifice - in humility and readiness to receive me as I am-- Ask of no man his blessings - his opinions - his favors -- Give unto Me credit for being that which I am - then I shall give unto thee in Greater Capacity ---

Before we continue - let it be understood that there are ones within flesh which hast the power and the authority to speak for me - in mine name -- For this have I ordained them as mine voice - mine hands made manifest -- Therefore I put mine words into their mouth - and they speak them -- As the Will of mine Father they are put into the mouth of mine priests and priestesses---

For that matter I Am the Will of Mine Father - and I give unto mine servants the power and the authority to speak in mine name - By the power and the authority invested in me - I have ordained this mine priestess - that she might do this mine work which I have allotted unto her -- For this have I prepared her - for she hast been a faithful and willing servant ---

I speak the WORD - she hears and obediently she performs the work I give unto her -- She fears no man - she gives no quarter - neither does she take any -- Blame not mine servant that this paper compares not to the learned letters of the intellectuals - for it is not mine intention to give unto thee a great and lengthy treatise on philosophy or science. And I have no intention to dwell on personalities -- I am come that ye be lifted up - that ye might be as one prepared to receive of the greater mysteries -- So be it that I am prepared to give unto thee as ye are prepared to receive-- Yet it is not yet time to reveal unto thee the "Greater Mysteries" which are neither written or spoken ---

I say: The "Greater Mysteries" are neither spoken nor written ---

Sori Sori -- Be ye blest this day and be ye as the hand of me made manifest unto them - and say unto them in mine name - that the way is prepared before them - and at no time have they been given the bitter cup -- For that matter they have prepared the bitter cup for themself - it is not of me ---

I am now prepared to give unto them the cup of Living Water -- It is said: The time is now come when they shall choose which way they go - it is so ---

I say: "Come Follow ME" - yet there are ones which sit as the poor in spirit moving not -- They are as the dead - they hear not neither do they stir ---

For this do I say awaken! Awaken!! - bestir thyself come forth - and follow me -- Wherein have they stirred?

I am the one which sees them in their lethargy and in their sleep -- It is a pitiful sight I see - for they know not that they stand on the brink of danger - I say "Danger" - I repeat: "They stand in danger!"

They shall be faced with great peril - for all is not well with them.

This is the time to awaken -- This the time to be up and about their preparation - for they shall enter into a place wherein they have not been - wherein there shall be great turmoil for the ones unprepared -- There shall be much confusion for the unprepared - the unstable - the poor in spirit - the ones which hast not been as the fortunate ones - the ones which have had the fortune to know that which is prepared before them ---

The Parable

I say: A table is prepared before thee - on that table is many things - (and that is not a mistake on my part)-- I say: "ON that table "IS" many things - and each shall be his own porter - he shall find on that table a portion which he is prepared to receive - for he hast created his own appetite -- His own mind is prepared to find that which he hast fortuned unto himself - therefore he shall find his own place - his own environment - and he shall in no wise be the better for his opinions - his lusts - his cravings - he shall find they have profited him naught ---

Yet he which puts away the passions - hate - lust and opinions - his pettiness - hypocrisy and malice - and follows where I lead - shall find thereon the fruit of Eternal Life ---

El Pater

Sori Sori -- Hast it not been said that great Light shall be shed upon the Earth? It is So - so shall it be ---

Now it is come when one shall go forth as one prepared - and he shall go as one in full armor -- He shall walk with men - he shall counsel men - and he shall bless them with his presence -- He shall carry with him the rod of power and authority - for I shall give unto him the authority and the power to speak in mine name - and he shall be as one submissive unto mine will - remembering always that I Am the Will of Mine Father made manifest ---

For this have I prepared him - for this have I called him forth and given unto him the name - which is El Pater -- This shall be his new name - and no man shall be unto him a barrier - neither shall they put him to shame - for he shall HONOR The Father - and he shall be just in all his dealings -- He shall fare well for I shall deal justly with him - and he shall remember from whence his calling -- He shall be as one mindful of the call - and he shall at no time betray himself ---

He shall begin his ministry now - and he shall waver not - for I have set mine Seal upon him -- I shall give unto him a number which shall be put within the palm of his hand - and it shall signify the number of days which are within the time left for the work at hand -- Yet no man shall decipher the meaning thereof - for I speak unto thee of the mysteries which no man can understand at this time -- Yet it shall be revealed unto him in the time to come -- Wherein is it said - there is a time unto all things -- I say: There is a season unto all things - a time of learning - a time of teaching - a time of going out - a time of coming in -- So be it there is a time of light - a time of darkness - plowing and sowing -- So be it that there is more to be said on that - yet it behooves thee to note that which I have said - ponder well mine Words ---

Ye shall make known that which I have said to El Pater - and he shall be alert - and prepare himself for the time draws nigh when I shall call him forth as one prepared to do a mighty work - and he shall do it with joy and gladness -- So be it and Selah ---

Sori Sori -- This day I would give unto thee this Word - and it shall be for the good of all -- So be it and Selah ---

Fortune thyself to hear me - and I shall give unto thee that which I have kept for thee - for thine own reward is kept for thee -- Thou knowest not that which I have kept for this day - when ye shall be as one prepared to receive it - it is that which thou hast not as yet dreamed nor asked ---

So be it I am prepared to give it - yet there is work to be done ere ye become one of the porters within the place of mine abode -- Howbeit thou hast gone out from mine place -- and it is said: Ye shall return -- So be it and Selah ---

Hold out thine hand and I shall touch it - and ye shall receive of me that which I have for them - and it shall profit them to receive it in mine name -- For this is mine time - mine word shall go out - and unto them which receiveth the WORD - unto them shall I show mine hand - I shall touch them and they shall know mine touch---

So be it I am not lacking in judgment - I am not lacking in wisdom, neither mercy or love - for mine love compares only to Mine Father's which hast sent me-- They know not the wisdom of mine actions in this. They comprehend not the judgment of mine acts - the mercy which I have upon them -- I say: Mine acts are three-fold - mine words are three-fold - and the Mighty Council hast prepared a part for each and every one which partakes of mine word -- They but have to accept it in mine name and abide by it - then they shall bear testimony of me - and they shall likewise be obedient unto the law -- They shall then be as one with each other - they shall not deny Mine "Servant" which hast been my diligent the handmaiden ---

These are the things which I would place before thee this day - and I say unto thee mine reader: Thou art not exempt from the law - no matter under which banner thou hast labored -- For thou art not as yet come into the fullness of thine estate - thou hast <u>not as yet</u> finished thine sojourn -- So be ye not puffed up - wear thine laurels not in peace - with satisfaction - for they deceive me not - I know that which thou hast done - I know that which is to do - and I come that it be done -- Rebel not against me - neither mine manner -- Resist not that which I bring forth in Wisdom -- Judge not mine Servants by that which I give unto them to do - for I am responsible for mine own acts -- I require from them Obedience - not perfection in all things! ---

I take the Obedience and use them as the Chalice - that I might fill it to the fill - that ye mine reader might be blest -- Think ye well upon this - for wherein hast thou heard mine Voice and followed me? Wherein hast thou prepared thineself to do mine work? Thinkest thou I do not Know thee? ---

It is said: "The harvest is Great and the reapers few" -- I say unto thee THIS DAY: The time is come when ye shall bow down thineself in holy supplication – and obedience - and willingness to do the Will of the Father-- Ye shall Surrender up thyself and falter not -- So be it I shall be thine witness - and no man shall deny thee thine inheritance - for I am the Keeper and the Guardian thereof ---

Sori Sori -- By the Grace of mine Father and by the efforts and Divine Director - hast this Great and Mighty Council been set up -- It is for the purpose of serving the Light - for the purpose of giving forth the law - which is the eternal verities ---

I am one of the Council -- For that matter I am head of the Council and it is said that there are numerous lodges - and sub-councils within or under of the Supreme Council ---

While men of Earth know little of the working of the Great and Mighty Council - they have set up their councils as poor imitations - as the lesser - for they know not the power - the ethic - the responsibility which goes with such as I speak of -- When I speak of the "Great and Mighty Council" it is the Organ thru which All the work for the system of planets is accomplished - thru and by the combined efforts of a dedicated company of <u>Personalities</u> - Yea - I say - personalities ---

While there are ones which would deny us personality - I say we do have personality - and individuality - with the Will (Combined Will) to serve the Light which never fails -- So be it I come as a member of this Council - in humility and with great love and wisdom --

I come with Great compassion for suffering humanity - the ones which are groping in darkness - the ones which have become lost in the maze of thinking and the forest which hold them bound -- They see not - for the shadows of the past hang deeply about them -- They lose their way - in the depth of despair they cry out - and I hear their cries -- Yet I reach out mine hand and they are so feeble of spirit - they reach not out to touch it ---

They sit in judgment on their fellowmen - while they do nothing to lift them up -- They forget from whence comes their help -- They <u>take,</u> giving no thot unto the ones which stand guard over them ---

This is the School of preparation - yet they refuse that which is placed before them -- They ask of <u>men</u> their opinions - their blessings and their alms - while all that is within our power we do - that they might become self-sufficient - I say: "THAT THEY BECOME SELF-SUFFICIENT"- that they might come into maturity - awaken unto their own potentials and become Sons of God-- This is offered unto each and every one which is capable of Eternal Life ---

Now it is come when the very gates of Heaven shall open up unto the ones prepared to enter therein ---

There shall be a great awakening!

For this am I come -- For this am I speaking -- For this shall I speak. I shall be heard!! ---

Now ye which hear me and give unto me credit for being that which I am - shall come to know me - and to bear witness of me - for I shall keep mine word – I shall not betray mine self - nor mine trust ---

Ye shall listen - and I shall speak -- Yet I say: Deceive not thineself - for I am not a petty priest - I am not a foolish nun -- I am a serious man - I am not a false god -- So I say unto thee: Be aware of me - and I shall give unto thee that which shall profit thee -- I shall stand Guard at thy gate - when thou hast cast aside thine puny ways and thine conceit, thine opinions - and offensive ways - that ye be prepared for mine part---

I bow unto no man -- I ask of none favors - yet I bow unto the light in every man - that which is Eternal within him -- I grovel not in the pit. I pray not unto any man that I receive sustenance from him - I KNOW wherein I am staid -- Therefore I say unto thee: Look and behold the Son of God - be ye even as he - and cast not lots for his garments - for they are even as nought unto thee -- I say - look ye well unto thine own - purify thineself that ye might walk the way in which I go - and this shall profit thee - for I shall bring thee into the place wherein I abide - therein is no darkness - no bondage --

Yet I say unto THEE: I am not favored - I am <u>not</u> favored - I am the one which hast become that which I wast created for to be -- So be it - and it is So - So shall it ever be ---

Sori Sori -- Such is mine word unto thee this day - for this mine word shall go forth that all might Know that which I say -- Mine word precedes me - where it is accepted in mine name there I am -- The word goes out before me that they might be prepared for to receive me ---

This is mine plan which no man can pilfer - neither shall he abort it for he knows not that which I shall do -- I shall do a new and strange thing which shall confound the ones which are not prepared to receive me ---

The way is prepared - and I come as a "thief in the night" while they sleep - and yet they sleep - knowing not the plan - neither of mine coming -- They go about asking of men their opinions - seeking of men their counsel - while I say: Come - Listen! Hear that which I say - yet they hear me not - they listen not!

Bear in mind I give not of mineself unto the unjust - the imprudent. I give unto them which seek that which I have for them -- I bless them which seek me out - which seek the Light which I am ---

There are ones which are now within the Earth (at this time) which are prepared to give unto thee the Cup of Living Water - and I am one of them -- Be ye as one prepared to receive - let it be - so shall it be ---

Forget not that the way hast been made strait before thee - and it is now come when ye shall follow in mine footsteps - and ye shall taste of the fruit of Eternal Life -- That is mine word for this day -- So be it I shall speak again and again --

The Test

Sori Sori -- Fortune thineself this part and it shall be placed within the foregoing letters - for they shall see and know that which I say unto thee ---

There are many which say this - and that - each adding his own opinion and embellishment -- Yet I have said unto thee: Ye shall not add one word or take away one word - ye shall give it unto them as ye receive it - and nothing shall be given unto them without the consent of the Mighty Council ---

For it is now come when many shall come forth declaring they are sent -- Yet I say they shall prove them self - yet no man shall demand of them proof - for they shall not satisfy man's demands for proof ---

Man shall find his proof in the word - and deed - yet he shall find that his deeds shall live after him - and his works shall be a living monument unto him - for he shall be as the one which hast been unto himself true---

Man shall demand proof - they shall look unto thee for proof - yet I say - he shall find none - for he shall not be satisfied -- Man shall test the word - by application of the law - he shall test that which I say - by application of the law ---

For this is the test I ask of him - this is his test - and ye shall exact none - for he shall test himself and grade himself - according unto his preparation-- None shall sit in judgment of him - neither shall any man sit in judgment of me or mine work - for I am he which hast come that he might Know wherein he is staid -- So be it I bring with me a mighty host - and they shall be as ones prepared for any and all occasions -- So be it and Selah ---

Sori Sori -- Say unto them which ask that there are ones which would distress them for the sake of bringing about the notice which they are apt to desire -- I say: There is great danger and stress - yet I ask that it be given unto them that they be prepared - for this is the whole desire of the company of which I am part ---

The ones which <u>would be</u> the prophet is but the one which knows not - the one which hast caused much fear - and anxiety ---

I say unto thee - I <u>Know</u> and I see that which the <u>would-be</u> prophet sees not - for mine vantage point is the Greater One -- Prepare thyself for changes - for changes are the order of the day -- Change is progress and progress is change -- So be it that there is no progress without change ---

For this do I say: Prepare thyself for the greater part - prepare thyself for change -- Be ye as one which can welcome change - and fortune thyself the new part - ever changing -- And waste not thine time looking backward - for I say unto thee - there are greater things in store than thou hast known -- There are greater things prepared for thee than thou hast ever had -- There are heights undreamed of - yet attainable.

Yet I say: Ye shall not look back - for to look back is to stumble -- There is a parable which says: Turn not back lest thou turn to a pillar of salt -- Know ye the meaning of that? While it is a simple saying - it behooves thee to ponder well its meaning ---

= **Blest is He** =

Be ye as the one pliable - acceptable unto me - and I shall lead thee into greater heights - greener pastures -- Greater glories shall be thine -- Ask not for small favors -- Bless thyself - for I say: "Blest is he which follows after me -- Blest is he which goes where I go -- Blest is he which goes all the way with me -- Blest is he which falters not -- Blest is he which hast received his inheritance -- Blest is he which hast upon his head the crown - and within his hand the Orb and the Scepter - for he hast overcome ---

By the counsel of the Great and Mighty Council shall they be prepared for the Greater Counsel -- They ask of men - yet I say - they receive not the greater from men - for men have not the power to open up the floodgates of Knowledge unto them -- For the greater comes not by word - neither the written pages ---

Not all their books contain the knowledge – wisdom – the learning which can be conveyed in one instant in and by the manner in which we reveal the secrets which are so mysterious unto them which seek.

= The Failure or Success of Prayer =

Yet they seek - they ask of whom - they look - but where - they say this and that - but what does it avail them -- Not all their mantras hast made them wise - neither hast their decrees cleansed them -- For the most part they pray unto a false god - an unknown god -- Wherein hast it been said: "They know not their Source" ---

When they call out in the name of the All Wise - All Powerful Father - SELFLESSLY - they shall be answered ---

I say: Pray ye not to be heard of men - or to receive their favor -- Pray ye that all men be lifted up -- So be it ye shall be heard ---

Now ye shall be as ones prepared to receive of the Greater mysteries for it is now come when they shall be revealed unto the just and the prudent ---

I say: Behold ye the hand of God move -- See it move - and know ye that it moves -- For by the hand of God shall these things be revealed unto thee -- This is the day of Revelation - the Revelation of Revelations - wherein ye shall have understanding of all former Revelations ---

For this have I put within thine hand these things of former ages -- Age after age - there hast been given revelation after revelation - yet not understood -- While I say unto thee this day - there shall now be understanding of the "former Revelations" -- So let there be understanding and wisdom ---

Howbeit that there are ones amongst thee which know not that I am come? ---

They have looked for one which would come in a cloud? Howbeit that they do not perceive the cloud? Howbeit they think there is no cloud??

I say I AM come! even in the "Cloud"! Yet they wait for one "Coming in a cloud"! While I say I am here - the cloud is heavy - and they know neither -- They see not for the cloud is dense - and their eyes blinded!

Yea - blind and deaf art they - for they see not - neither do they hear.

While the WORD is placed before them - it is not comprehended.

I am speaking that they might have comprehension -- I shall speak unto them in ways which are new and strange -- I shall write upon their heart that which they shall not forget -- I shall do a wondrous thing - and I shall be as the Author and finisher of mine work - for no man shall abort the plan of which I speak ---

I am the Host of Hosts and I bring with me mighty warriors - long trained in the way of the just and prudent -- I know them to be trustworthy - and they are Mighty - endowed with power and Wisdom!

They have not taken up residence upon the Earth - they are free from all bonds - all bounds -- They are bound by no law save that of "Love" which motivates their every act -- They know the Earth - all the systems of Earth - man - animal - plants - yea the thots of every one - every living thing they know well -- They know the composition of all things -- I say - there is no secrets - for they are learned in their part - they are learned in the schools far beyond man's comprehension - and at no time shall man put them to shame ---

I tell thee of a truth - they art thy Superiors -- Think ye not that thou art wise O man! for thou art lower than the "Angels" - thou hast as yet not seen that which ye shall become - for thou art within a "low grade" and I say unto thee: "Come forth" - and ye move not - for thou art in lethargy ---

I stand ready to assist thee when ye pick up thine feet - and reach out thy hand that I might touch it -- Be ye not deceived in this - I say try me ---

I say: Pick up thy feet - seek me out - look unto ME - ask of Me - be ye as one SELFLESS - and I shall walk with thee all the way ---

I give not mineself unto the unjust and imprudent - I bow down unto the just and prudent -- I go not into the den of the dragon - yet I go down into the bottomless pit to find the just and the humble -- I bow down unto the ones which give of themself that others be lifted up ---

I give not unto the bigot and braggard - for they find their reward in the plaudits of men -- They find their reward in man's flattery - and wherein hast it profited them -- I say unto them: Thou fool - what hast it profited thee -- I am come that ye be not deceived - of men - for their flattery is liken unto the tack in thine shoe ---

Blest art they which shuns man's flattery - and finds his reward in selfless service - asking nought of man - yea - such is the reward of the Servant -- The reward which is everlasting - and outshining a King's diadem is that which I offer thee -- I say: Come follow ye me and I shall show thee many things which thou hast not seen ---

I promise thee NOT fame - nor fortune -- I promise thee freedom - even as I am free -- Think ye that I am an imposter asking of thee favor?

I say unto thee: I bow down mineself that ye be lifted up! So be it that ye shall give unto me credit for being that which I AM - and I shall show unto thee that which thou hast not seen-- I promise thee <u>not</u> miracles - I promise thee Eternal Freedom - this shall profit thee -- Wherein hast there been a man amongst thee which hast given unto thee that which delivered thee -- I say there hast not been one -- Even though he hast been as one mild and gentle - he hast not been unto thee the deliverer - he hast not been unto thee Savior ---

I say - to save thyself is the greater wisdom -- A man goeth unto the rescue of a drowning man - and knoweth not how to swim perisheth also -- So be it I say: First pick up thine own feet - and they shall be shown the way - for I have opened up the way - and for this am I the Wayshower ---

Place thine hand in mine and I shall lead thee gently - and I shall deal justly with thee - for I know thine needs - thine frailties -- Yet I say: <u>YE</u> shall overcome thine weakness - for I shall give unto thee as thou art prepared to receive ---

Let this go down in history as I have spoken it - for it is spoken for a reason - and a time -- This shall conclude the "Part of Counsel" - and we shall enter it into the records -- Therefore they shall have it available as they are prepared to receive it -- Then another shall follow this part "The Part of Counsel"-- This next part shall be "The Part of Wisdom" and it shall profit them to accept it in Mine Name - for I say - as they accept mine WORD - and mine servant - so do they receive me ---

I say: Bear ye in mind - I am he which is Sent to bear witness of Mine Father -- Likewise do I send mine word out - <u>by</u> mine servants - that they bear witness of me -- Unto them which receive them in mine name I say: Behold ye me - and I shall touch thee and ye shall be quickened - and ye shall know as I Know ---

Bear ye in mind that I am bound by mine word - and mine word is valid -- No man shall invalidate it -- So be it I am come that it be brot forth this day - the plan - which is given unto me - and I shall do mine part ---

Let it be said: Thou hast done thine ---

Let it be said: Thou hast been true unto thine trust ---

Blest art they which are trustworthy ---

Blest art they which are prepared to receive me -- Blest art they which are with me -- Blest art they which go all the way with me -- So be it I shall give unto them as I have received of mine Father - for He hast empowered me with the authority to give unto thee <u>just</u> as I have received - and I have received mine inheritance in full -- So be it and Selah ---

This concludes "The Part of Counsel"

- - -

"The Part of Wisdom" follows –

THE PART OF WISDOM

Sori Sori -- By the Mighty Council shall ye receive this part - and it shall be added unto the part of Counsel - which hast gone before -- This shall be as the Part of Wisdom ---

Blest art they which receive this part - and blest art thou that ye receive it unto thineself ---

Praise be the Lord of Hosts -- Praise ye the Name of Solen Aum Solen ---

Let thine Voice be as the Voice of the Lord thy God - and say that which he puts into thy mouth - and thine hand shall do that which he gives unto thee to do-- So let it be - let it be for the good of all -- Amen and Selah ---

Fortune thyself the reward which goes after obedience -- Let not thine left hand know that which the right hand doeth - for I say unto thee: Thine hand shall be turned up - and it shall be filled - and it shall be as the Great and Mighty Council hast filled it -- For it is now come when there shall be a Mighty Change in the complexion of thy work -- Hear ye me: A Great change shall be brot about - and it shall serve the people of this day - for the need is Great - and the need shall be filled - I am come that it be filled ---

Now I say unto them: The time is come when ye shall put into practice that which hast been given unto thee concerning the LAW - concerning thine salvation and thine Mighty Inheritance ---

Bear in mind that there is but one Father Solen Aum Solen - One Lord of Lords - One I say! Yet there is a Mighty Host which bears witness of Him - and that I shall speak of later -- Let thine works bear witness of me - for I come that ye might do the work which I do -- So let it profit thee - for as thou art prepared so shall ye receive ---

Hear ye - I say: "As thou art prepared so shall ye receive" ---

This I would have thee understand - <u>there</u> <u>is</u> <u>a</u> <u>plan</u> - and it is given unto me to know the fullness thereof -- While ye know not but part - yea - a very small part indeed - for man comprehends but a small part of the Whole Plan - his comprehension is indeed <u>puny</u> ---

While I say I know the plan - I say it behooves thee to do the will of the Father which hast sent me - for I come by and thru His Will which I Am ---

When thou hast so prepared thineself for to receive me - then I shall give unto thee a part new and powerful - and ye shall go forth as one qualified to do mine work -- Yet I say: I send not a boy to do a man's work!

Behold in me the Light of the World -- Behold in me the law - which I am - and qualify thyself to receive as I have received ---

Let thine garments be white as snow -- Let thine hands be clean -- Let thine words be mine words -- Let thine time be mine time -- Walk ye in the way I shew thee - and be ye not fearful - for I shall lead thee in the path of righteousness all the days of thine life -- Let thine feet be swift to do mine bidding -- Let thine ways be the way of righteousness Bear ye no false witness - for or against any man -- Be ye as one alert Watch thine tongue -- Be ye alert that ye put not thine foot into a hole

Watch! Watch! and pray diligently - and be ye as one obedient unto mine touch -- For it is now come when I shall touch them which have gone all the way with me -- Number thine steps - count them well-- I ask of thee how far hast thou gone with me? Hast thou gone all the way?

When it is come that thou standeth with me upon mine high Holy Mount - then ye shall see and know as I know - Then ye shall Know that which is meant by "PREPARE" -- The word signifies little - it is the preparation which brings thee forth out of bondage -- It is the preparation - that brings thee understanding - and not one which hast prepared themself is denied that which they prepare themself for to receive ---

Let it be said: The lawyer prepares himself for to be a lawyer - and the physician prepares himself for to be a physician -- The plowman likewise prepares himself for to prepare the ground for the seed ---

I say: I am the Lawyer - and Mine hand wields the Sword -- By the hand of one prepared - ye are given this mine word - for She is a "plowman" -- She goes before me to prepare the ground -- And I say: I am the Keeper of the records - I know what is written in the "Book of Life" - and I know that which thou hast done - and the part which hast been given unto thee -- I too say that the plowman goes before the sower and prepares the ground - and as it is prepared - the seeds are placed therein according unto the likeness of the seed - according unto the preparation of the ground to receive the seed -- This is all according unto the law -- And it is for this that I say: I send mine plowmen before me - that the ground be prepared for that which I have -- For there is little time - the harvest shall be upon thee - and there shall be a gathering in -- And I ask of thee: Where dost thou stand - of what account - of what hast thou - that thou canst boast??

I ask of thee: What bringeth forth thou O man -- What is thine offering - thine talent - thine sacrifice-- What hast thou to offer up unto the Altar of the Living God - the Father Solen Aum Solen?

I say: BRING THINESELF as the only acceptable sacrifice -- Surrender up thine puny self in holy surrender - asking no reward - no glory - and praise ye the Father for His Goodness and Mercy - for He shall be unto thee all things -- Seek ye the Light which I Am - and be ye as one prepared to receive in great measure -- So let it be ---

Sori Sori -- This would I say unto thee: Be ye as one which I have touched - and be ye as one prepared for the greater part - for I shall come in and abide with thee - and ye shall be as mine hand made manifest unto them ---

They shall be as ones prepared to receive the Word and they shall be blest to receive it in mine name -- So be it and Selah ---

This I would say unto them this day: Not all their letters - books - libraries - their schools of learning are sufficient unto their learning this day -- For I have come that they might learn of me - that which hast not been found in their schools - colleges - their institutions of learning -- It is said: The letter killeth - the letter without the Spirit is dead -- I come that ye have Light - that the letter might have meaning -- So let it be said: I am the Spirit - I am the Word made manifest -- So be it and Selah ---

Wherein is it said that the ones which accept mine word shall accept me -- First they shall accept the <u>Word</u> - then mine servant - <u>then</u> I shall reveal unto them mineself - then I shall be unto them Sibor -- While they shall first receive of mine servant as they would of me - they shall love mine servant as they would love me - and then they shall come to know me -- So be it that I go not out before mine servant - I send mine servant out before me - and they shall herald mine coming---

Such is mine word unto them which await mine coming -- I say: I AM COME -- While ye wait - I am about mine Father's business -- I am not alone - for I bear testimony of a multitude which are with me - And they are staunch - they are aware of thine needs - and weakness -- They are not amongst the dead - they are of the Light -- They are not of the darkness - they are as the Mighty Sons of God -- They are fully aware of their part - and they waver not - neither shall they be found wanting ---

I say unto thee: Be ye as one which has ears to hear that which I say unto thee - for by thine own light shall I find thee -- By thine own works shall ye be judged -- Let it be said that as thou art prepared - so shall ye receive ---

While it is said: "Many are called and <u>few</u> are chosen" - it is because <u>they</u> are not as ones prepared that they are rejected -- The ones which are found worthy to receive me - and of me - are <u>not</u> rejected -- While they may turn aside at any time - they are not the one bound as slaves - they are free to choose - they are given free will - and there is no penalty put upon them for receiving me -- They choose me - and I am he which hast said: "Come unto me and I shall make light thine burdens" - and it is so ---

I too say: I am come that ye be delivered out of bondage -- Wherein hast it been said that ye shall give of <u>thyself</u> - for none other gift shall I accept -- I ask not that ye give unto me coin of thy realm -- I ask that ye give unto mine servant that he be fed and clothed - while he serves me with his whole heart and hand -- While it is given unto him to receive of me - he shall receive of thee that which shall feed and clothe. his mortal body ---

I say: Blest is the one which feeds and clothes mine servant while he serves me -- So be it that I have watched thee - I know thine capacity and I know thine weakness -- Yet it is said: "Thine weakness shall be overcome - and thine capacity shall be increased"-- So let it be - for this do I now speak -- Let thine capacity be increased - and according unto thy capacity shall ye receive - so be it the law ---

Be ye as the hand of me made manifest - and give unto them this part - that they might be prepared - for as ye give so shall ye receive -- Be it so - so shall it be -- It is now come when they shall say: It is repeated thus and so -- Yet I ask of them: What hast thou done with that which I have given unto thee? -- I ask of thee: Hast thou profited thineself -- Hast thou been true unto thineself - hast thou picked up thine feet - hast thou examined thineself??

What profit it a man should he know the time of his going out - when he hast not prepared himself?

What profiteth a man - should he know the time of his departure from the Earth should he not know wherein he is bound? What profiteth a man should he know the weight of the Earth - should he not know his own weight?

Now I say unto thee: I speak unto thee concerning thine own salvation - and this is that which thou art prone to neglect -- I say: Thou hast concerned thineself with the ways of men and animals - and they have prepared for thee many a bitter cup -- While I say: "Seek ye the Light" - and ye know me not ---

Ye turn unto man and ask of him - while I stand before thee imploring thee --

While I stand as one prepared to give unto thee as I have received of Mine Father ---

Be ye as one prepared to accept me and that which I have kept for thee ---

It is with great love that I come unto thee - for the purpose of bringing thee out of bondage ---

Be ye aware of me - mine presence - and I shall give unto thee comprehension -- Yet I say unto thee: BE YE NOT DECEIVED - for I go not into the fowler's snare - I go not where angels fear to tread -- Cleanse thine house - and I shall come in and sup with thee -- So be it it shall profit thee ---

Wherein is it said that I shall do a wondrous work? and it is so - for I shall give unto the little ones power to build mighty mansions -- I shall raise up the simple to do the work of the wise -- I shall put mine words into the mouth of the dumb -- I shall loosen the tongue of the "spastic". I shall open the ears of the deaf - and make swift the feet of the halt and the lame - for I shall deliver them from their bondage -- I shall do ALL these things - and more!

While it is a small thing which I say I shall do - for I am one of action - and that which I shall do is beyond thy mortal concept -- For man hast not yet conceived of the vastness of mine part -- He hast thot of me as <u>having been</u> - <u>Come</u> and <u>gone</u> -- Yet he knows not - wherefrom I come - neither where I went - nor that which I AM DOING -- I say unto thee: Come - open up thine eyes - thine ears - lift up thine hand -- Thine heart shall be opened up - and ye shall be given as thou art prepared to receive -- While it is said many times: "Prepare thyself for the greater part" - I ask of thee: For what art thou prepared? Hast thou given of <u>thineself</u> hast thou surrendered up thine will? Hast thou put aside thine puny ways - hast thou cast from thee all thine preconceived ideas of me and about me? Hast thou brot unto the altar thineself as a LIVING sacrifice?

Behold the Light! Look ye unto no man for thine salvation - ask of no man - for I say unto thee: <u>Prepare</u> thineself for to receive of me - and I shall reveal unto thee all that ye have need of -- Let it be that I find thee prepared -- So be it I am come as a thief in the night -- Let it be said of thee: Thine light burns upon the altar of life - for it is by thy light that I shall find thee ---

Be ye as one on whose shoulders is placed thine own responsibility. None other shall bear thine cross - for thou art responsible for all thine deeds - words and acts -- While it is said: Thine "Savior" is come - I say: the way I have set before thee - I have come that the way be prepared -- Yet I cannot atone for one man -- Mine part is to show the way unto Mine Father's House-- While it is given unto me to come as the "Wayshower" - I say: It is for thine own good that I come -- Not that I might atone for thy "Sins" nor shortcomings---

I say: Be ye aware of mine words! - be ye as one alert - and crawl not on thine belly for man's favors -- Hold high thine head - see the works of the Lord thy God - and prostrate thineself in humility before God the Father - that He might be glorified in thee ---

Let it be said that humility is the step to the door of His House - the step on which thou shall wait - until thou hast learned the final lesson of love divine---

Blest are the humble of heart -- Thrice blest are they which love Divinely -- So be it - it is for mine love that I return unto thee this day. Turn not away - for it is for thine own sake that I come - for mine Great love - and compassion of a world in bondage -- Blest am I that I am given the privilege of serving the Light this day -- Yet I say: This is not the first nor the last of mine service - for I shall always continue to serve mine Father in the capacity given unto me -- Therein is mine reward - joy -- For service unto the Father is the Greatest joy of man - for He is the Giver of all good gifts - and all according unto the preparation - thy preparation -- Be ye as one prepared to receive of Him as I have received -- So be it that I have received mine inheritance in full ---

Hold ye high the banner of freedom - forch not that which ye have on any man -- Bless him by the word and deed -- Give of "thyself" that he be led aright - let him see thy light -- Yet ye shall not forch upon him thine preachments - opinions - ideas - nor "Way of life." ---

Let it be given unto thee to show forth that which thou hast been given -- Let thine own deeds - and acts be thy testimony of thy innermost convictions -- Let not thy lips make of thee a liar -- Fortune thyself that which shall profit thee -- Let not thine brother fall upon thine spear - for I say - he shall walk by thine lamp -- Keep it oiled and clean -- Prepare ye the way of the Lord - for he is now <u>Come</u> - and he shall be as a guest within thine house but a short while - yet with thee he shall abide -- Always should there be a place for him -- Let it be prepared - and he shall enter in and fellowship with thee - and sweet shall it be -- So let it be --

Boast not of thine virtue - be ye as one humble of spirit -- Let thine Light <u>shine</u> - and give unto no man the bitter cup -- Sup with me and thine lips shall be as the petal of the rose - soft unto the touch - and the fragrance shall be sweet - for no scorching words shall escape from them to betray thine innermost being-- I say: Keep thine tongue - and let only words of love and peace escape from them -- Hold thine wrath, subdue thine passions - give in wisdom - and withhold not thine love - that which shall profit thine fellowmen -- Give without stint - yet ye shall be as one prudent and wise in thine giving -- For many shall put their foot into a hole while going forth to do a good deed - for the unjust and imprudent will take from thee thine fortune and cast thee into prison! I say: Beware of the unjust - the idol-worshipers - the infidel - the gossiper - the whoremongers and the hypocrite - for they are the ones which are clothed in garments as man - they wear the cloak of flesh - and would deceive thee ---

I say: Be ye not deceived by appearance - for they would deceive thee -- Let it be said now - that "All is not gold that glistens" - neither is the glass the diamond - yet it sends forth its rays -- While the diamond is of little worth - I say a gentle man/ woman - is to be sought for the worth ---

Be ye as one which sees the light within - and cast from thee the wicked as ye would the dog which hast his filth upon him -- For I say - the wicked ye have with thee -- While I say - the righteous shall be unto thee companion and friend - thy brother - and helper -- Fear not the wicked - give him no quarter - pass him by - let him not snare thee - for he is cunning in his ways - and he plays his flute before thee -- A thousand tunes he plays that ye might follow him - be ye as one alert unto his cunning - and give him no ear ---

Be ye as one prepared to enter into the holy of holies - for therein ye shall know as I know -- Ye shall abide by the law which I bring - and ye shall walk in the way I set before thee - for I come that ye be set aright - that ye walk upright/ honorable in the sight of Mine Father which hast Sent Me -- So be it I bear witness of Him - and I am come that ye might receive of Him even as I have received -- So let it profit thee to follow after me ---

I am he which is Sent that ye be delivered out ---

= Life - - Death =

Sori Sori -- This word I would have thee give unto them which seek the Light -- For this do I give it unto thee this day ---

Bear ye in mind that there is no death - All is life - life - I say - ALL IS LIFE -- There is no death in reality - death is but a state of life -- The life which is the Life - is first and last - always penetrating ALL Substance - even unto the end -- While the Substance changes - the life which animates the Substance changes not -- It is given unto me to know the law governing all substance and the changes thereof -- For this have I said: "I shall show thee Greater things"- and it is so -- While I say - I shall shew unto thee greater things - I say: Prepare thineself for to learn of me - for I am he which cometh into the darkness that ye have light -- Be ye as ones aware of that which I bring that which I do - and give unto me credit for being that which I am – I AM ---

Now ye shall fortune unto thyself greater learning - and a greater fortune - for it behooves thee to put out thy hand that ye receive of me. I say: Thou hast been slothful and negligent in thine search - for thou hast searched in places afar off - in thy libraries - in the places of darkness -- Yet I say: I am nearer than thy hands and feet -- I Am here, I am there - I AM Come - that ye might awaken unto me - and come alive -- Awaken - and know thyself to be one with me ---

I bid thee arise! Come forth! Stand ye upright and speak the words of Life - and ye shall be heard and I shall attend thee - so let it be ---

Be ye as one which can stand firm in the face of adversity -- Let thine adversaries turn and flee from thee - for I say unto thee - they shall have no power over thee -- Be ye as one on whose head I have placed mine hand - and give unto them nothing which they can use against thee -- Yet I say unto thee: "Blest art they which suffer persecution for mine sake" -- Let them speak their piece - yet it shall not move thee - for I have given unto thee that which shall suffice thee in the hours of persecution -- Let it be said that I am with thee unto the end -- So be it I have called thee forth as mine hand and I shall do a strange and wondrous act! –

SO LET IT BE as I have spoken - for I say - it shall be strange unto them - yet for this shall ye be prepared ---

So be it I am the one which keeps mine own counsel - and I am not bound by any man's opinions - neither do I ask aught of <u>any</u> man -- While I say unto ALL: Come and follow me - they shall come of their own free will - for none shall bring them against their will ---

I say: They which follow me shall be as ones free from all bondage. So be it they which wait shall cry out in their pity and confusion - their torment - and they shall wait -- While their waiting shall be hard - I say it shall be hard - yet they have made it so ---

Be ye as one which hast heard me - and I say ye shall be as one responsible for all thine ways - all thine misdeeds -thine "Sins" - thine erroneous ways -- While ye shall say: Lord! Lord! many times - it is not sufficient -- Ye shall do that which I have given unto thee to do -- It is clearly stated and written many times - yet ye weary of mine sayings - and ye become impatient with them which serve me as mine hands and feet --

Thou hast not been unto them mindful -- Thou hast asked for <u>self</u> - and the law is exacting -- It is not given unto one to atone for the errors of another -- Correct thine own weakness and shortcomings -- Submit unto the Father thy will - and I shall come unto thee and prepare thee for another part - greater than thou hast known. Be ye as one prepared to receive of me as I have received of Mine Father ---

I say unto thee: The way is clearly marked before thee - thou hast been given the law - thou hast had the "Word" - thou hast been as one which hast been brot forth this day for to be that which the Father would have thee be ---

Now I ask of the only one thing - be ye as one prepared to stand before Him as a Son of God made perfect in me - for in Him I Am - and I am come that ye become A Son of God -- So let it be as He hast Willed it ---

I come not to bear false testimony -- I come not to give unto thee great and fancy opinion or lengthy sermons -- I come that I might bring thee out of bondage - that ye might return unto mine Father with me -- So be it that I bear witness of Him which is the CAUSE of thine being. He which is Solen Aum Solen - and He shall be as the Solen Aum Solen forever and forever - so be it and Selah -- Amen and Amen - forever and forever ---

Sori Sori -- Fortune thyself the greater part - for I come that ye receive thine inheritance in full -- So let it be said that I am the Lord of Lords - the Host of Hosts - and the One Sent of mine Father that it be done -- There is but one Lord God - One Father Solen Aum Solen - and I am one with mine Father -- He hast sent me that His Will be made manifest -- So shall it be for I am come as His Will -- So be it I say unto all: Look up - See - and Know that which is given unto thee to do - for it is now come when there shall be great light flood the Earth - for I bring with me a host of workers which know the law -- They are prepared to execute it for the <u>Good</u> of All ---

= Behold the Bee =

Now I say: Great changes shall take place - and they shall be as the law demands - for it is given unto man to be in need of change ---

The time is come when there shall be a division - the workers shall be separated from the drones - and the drones shall no longer be as ones which usurp the fortune of the workers -- Wherein is it said that the workers shall be as the ones prepared to receive me and of me -- I say: The "drones" shall be the sleepers - the ones which do not the work at hand --They shall be as the "DRONES" which produce not ---

The time is come for the workers to find that which they have sought so fervently - while the drones - and the unfortunate one shall be turned out ---

I say: Behold the Bee - see the plan - and know ye there is a plan - and none shall let his feet drag -- So be it I see them laggardly sit and ask of others that they be comforted -- So be it I say unto thee: Behold the BEE! Too - I say: I shall do a mighty work - and I shall find them which are prepared to do mine work -- I say: I ask not the <u>boy</u> to do the work of a man - - for he hast not the capacity ---

See ye the plan - let it be as planned - for as they are prepared so shall they receive -- Be ye aware of that which is being done - let it be. For this do I say unto thee: Let it be- let it be!! - For this do I say unto thee fear not - I am with thee - and I am not a puny god - I am he which is sent that there be Light - So let it be ---

By the Word shall ye be made whole -- By the Word shall ye be made perfect -- Therefore I say unto thee: Receive of me - for I am the WORD made flesh -- I am <u>he</u> which is come into flesh - and flesh contaminates me not -- Be ye as one prepared to stand with me and bear witness of mine Father Which hast Sent ME --

So be it I am His Will made flesh -- I Am <u>His</u> hand - His Voice - and I do that which He would have me do -- So be it and Selah ---

Fortune thineself such joy as I know - for I have received of Him the Father Solen Aum Solen mine inheritance in full - and no man shall say me nay -- For I am he which hast been about mine Father's business for long - while thou O man - hast slept for long ---

Now I say: Awake! Awaken unto ME --- Arise - come forth and accept that which I have for thee -- I have said that I shall do mine part when thou hast done thine -- When thou hast prepared thyself I shall come unto <u>thee</u> - and I shall do that which I have said I shall do - for I am <u>not</u> the deceiver! ---

I shall prove mineself -- Be ye as the little child - reach out thy hand and I shall lead thee into fields afar -- I shall shew thee things undreamed of -- Ye shall see and know that which hast mystified thee and all things shall be unto thee clear - for the "Myst" shall be cleared away - ye shall no more wander in darkness ---

Behold -- I say: Behold the Hand of God - See It move - and ye shall Know it moves with Wisdom - and with power -- So be it I say unto <u>thee</u>: Hold ye steadfast - for there are ones which would trample thee - which would put thee down to rise no more! ---

Be ye as one alert and give unto me credit for being that which I am. So be it that I am he which is come that there be light - so let it be.

Blest are They

By the hand of God art thou sustained -- By the hand of God art thou sustained -- By the hand of God art thou sustained ---

Blest are they which See the hand of God move ---

Blest are they which See the hand of God move ---

Blest are they which are prepared for the Greater Vision ---

Blest are they which are prepared for the Greater Vision ---

Blest are they which are prepared for the Greater Vision ---

Blest are they which come into the fullness of their inheritance ---

Blest are they which come into the fullness of their inheritance ---

Blest are they which come into the fullness of their inheritance ---

Blest are they for they shall go into bondage no more ---

Blest are they for they shall go into bondage no more ---

Blest are they for they shall go into bondage no more ---

Blest are they for they shall Know God the Father---

Blest are they for they shall Know God the Father---

Blest are they for they shall Know God the Father---

Blest are they which Know Him for they shall abide with Him forever - and forever ---

Blest are they which Know Him for they shall abide with Him forever ---

Blest are they which Know Him for they shall abide with Him forever ---

Blest are they which abide with Him for they shall be like Him ---

Blest are they which abide with Him for they shall be like Him ---

Blest are they which abide with Him for they shall be like Him ---

Blest are they which are like Him ---

Blest are they which are like Him ---

Blest are they which are like Him ---

I AM - - I AM - - I AM - - -

I AM - - I AM - - I AM - - -

I AM - - I AM - - I AM - - -

Sori Sori -- By the hand of God shall ye be led out of bondage ---

By the hand of God shall ye be brot into the place wherein He abides ---

By the hand of God shall ye be born again.

By the hand of God shall ye receive thy Orb and thy Scepter.

By the hand of God shall ye be made Whole.

By the hand of God shall ye be brot back unto thine rightful estate.

By the hand of God shall ye be at One with the Father Solen Aum Solen ---

For He hast sent thee out as Perfect in the beginning that ye might return unto Him even as ye went forth -- I say: Ye shall return unto Him PERFECT - even as He created thee - "PERFECT" ---

I am come this day that it be so -- So let it be as He hast Willed it. Amen and Amen -- Behold ye the hand of God move -- I see it move. I Know the movements thereof - and I behold the perfection of the plan. So shall it be revealed unto thee in the day of thy preparation.

The preparation is the way in which ye overcome the darkness and imperfection which thou hast fortuned unto thyself -- I say - cast from thee all darkness - throw off the yoke - be ye as one free to follow me. I shall lift thee up - and I shall be unto thee all the Father would have me be - for this is mine part - I shall be His hands and feet made manifest - for He is manifest in me - I in Him -- We are One - So be it and Selah ---

The Great Mirror

Bear ye in mind that there is little time left unto thy preparation - for it is given unto each to have a day - a number - and when that day comes, the number called - ye shall respond to the call - and no man shall stay thee -- I say - no man shall set aside a day on which ye shall appear before the Great Mirror - and see thyself as thou art -- So let it be understood that which I have said is for thy own sake - for I am come solely for my love for thee ---

O ye children of Earth! I say unto thee: Thou Knowest not that which is in store for thee -- Arise! and come forth - that ye might be found worthy of thine mighty inheritance -- Pray that ye be found worthy! ---

Wait - learn of me - and ask of me - and I shall touch thee and ye shall Know that which I have said to be TRUTH -- So be it I say unto thee: Seek ye the Light which I Am -- Love ye one another -- Bless him which gives unto thee truth and light -- Bless him which gives unto thee food and drink -- Bless him which gives unto thee shelter -- Bless him which leads thee aright -- Bless him which goes the last mile with thee. Bless him which comforts thee in the time of stress ---

Yet I say unto thee: Seek no favors of men -- Ask nought of man - for he hast not as yet received his freedom -- I am the "bondsman" - I come that ye be delivered out of bondage -- I await thy call -- Blest are they which receive me - for I shall minister unto them as I have been administered unto ---

Be ye not critical of mine words - mine way - for I say unto thee - I Know that which I am about -- I come that ye be lifted up - that ye be UN-BOUND! So let it be -- For thine own sake do I speak thusly -- Look - See - Listen - Hear - Do - Act - and become that which shall be the Will of The Father -- Bless thyself ---

The Risen Christ

Sori Sori -- For the day at hand - let it be said that there are many which sit in waiting - watching for mine approach -- I say unto them which <u>wait</u>: Wait no more! for I AM COME! I AM COME - I AM COME - be ye alert unto mine presence - for I Am here! ---

I say: I Am here -- At no time shall I show mine wounds unto any man - for I am done with the wounds -- I shall not bare mine breast unto any man - that he put his fingers into the wounds - for I say: I come not as the slain priest -- I come as the "RISEN CHRIST" -- I come as the VICTOR -- I come as the Son of God Victorious!

Be ye mindful of the prize - the crown - the victor wears -- Let the past be done - finished - I say <u>finished</u>!! - and turn not back - for I say: I Am the Risen Lord - the Victor - the one which hast won the Victory. I bid thee follow me - and I shall give unto thee the portion which I have kept for thee -- Wait no more - for I say unto thee: The time is come when I shall make known mineself - and feign not the power to see - when it is not so - for I am not deceived -- Deceive not thyself by false concepts and imagings -- I say: Ye shall not image me - for I shall come unto thee as thou art prepared to receive me -- So be it and Selah.

Wherein hast thine imaginations profited thee?

So be it I am not an image - save that of Mine Father -- So be it His image is perfect - for this have I come that ye might know the perfect image which is His -- For man creates his images imperfectly - they are poor likeness of the perfect one - which is that which changes not ---

Behold the perfect ONE - the Radiant ONE - for I am come that ye be transformed into the perfect image of the perfect ONE ---

Behold the One made in His likeness - for I say unto thee - there is but the ONE perfect - and He is the Father which hast Sent me ---

As His hand and foot I am come -- I am ONE with Him and in Him. I am One made in His image - made perfect am I -- So be it and Selah.

Sori Sori -- Bear ye in mind - I am come unto thee that ye might bear witness of me - and at no time hast thou denied me or mine word.

Now I say unto thee: Ye shall walk with me as a living testimony of me and mine work ---

So be it that I shall give unto thee a part which is separate from all others - for thou hast prepared thyself for a part which is unlike that of any other - for I say unto thee - it hast been given unto thee to have a part which differs from all others -- And that shall be as another book - separate and apart from that which is now being written - for this is for them which would be prepared - for them which are waiting ---

Now it is come upon thee - that they shall be as the ones to receive this mine word - yet few there be which shall be prepared to receive that which I shall give unto thee - - which shall follow after this book of "Wisdom" -- Let it be said - this is but the beginning of their preparation - and as they are prepared so shall they receive -- So be it and Selah ---

I say unto thee mine beloved: Ye shall give this unto them - and when it is come that they have proven themself - they shall find that they shall receive in greater measure -- So be it that I have said so - so shall it be -- Let it be for their own sake that they shall be prepared - it shall be for their own sake -- Therefore I say unto thee: Let thine hand be mine - thine hand shall be swift to do mine work - and it shall be accurate and it shall not fail ---

By the hand of God made manifest shall this work be completed - and it shall find its mark -- And no man shall stay the hand of God which directs its flight - as the arrow shall it go forth - swift in its flight and sure of its mark -- So be it and Selah ---

Sori Sori -- By the hand of the Almighty God shall this be recorded and for all time shall it be - for the time now comes when man shall see the fallacy of his opinions and preconceived ideas -- I say: He shall <u>see</u> the fallacy of his opinions and ideas - for he hast formed many opinions erroneously - and incorrect they are - for they know me not ---

They have made images of me - and they have put their foot against me - for it is said - they shall not serve two masters -- So be it I ask nought of them - save obedience unto the law - the law by which I have proven mineself worthy to be called "Son of God" -- So let it suffice <u>them</u> - for as I have received so shall they receive - when they do that which I do -- I come that they might learn of ME that which shall be unto them the law which shall free them of ALL Earthly bondage -- While I say - I come that they have <u>light</u> - I say - they spurn me - and that which I give unto them -- Fear ye no man - and be thine own porter. Let no man bind thee - for I come that ye be free -- Yet there is work to be done - and at no time shall ye ride mine back-- I say: Pick up thy feet and stand erect -- Let not thy feet drag - walk ye after me - walk ye in the way I point -- Bear ye in mind that thy responsibility lies upon thine own shoulders -- None else shall be responsible for thee -- <u>Prepare thyself</u> - I say: Prepare - and I shall draw nigh unto thee - and I shall give unto thee as thou art prepared to receive -- So be it and Selah ---

I speak unto thee simply - plainly - and clearly - for I am not of a mind to confound thee with great phrases and fine words to <u>please</u> thee. I say: I know that which is needful - I say - pay ye heed unto the WORD, let the <u>letter be</u> - for it shall profit thee naught ---

Be ye aware of the WORD/ the law - and I shall shew thee many things thou hast not seen -- I say ye shall be as one obedient unto the law - even as mine priestess is obedient unto me - for she asks nought of thee - save that of obedience - that is the law: as ye <u>give</u> so shall ye receive -- Pity are they which have turned me out -- Pity are they which know me not -- Pity are they which hear me not -- Pity are they which cast out mine servants ---

Pity are they which bring unto me their petitions for self-appetites, for self-gratification - and these do I see as ones bowed before their altars - crying out for things of flesh - and for things of the world - asking alms and favors of men -- Yet they have not asked of the Father for that which shall profit them ---

I say: They ask for things which shall pass away - yet they know not that which He hast endowed unto them -- Pity I say - are the ones which seek of men the things which pass away -- Pity are they for they are as ones bound in darkness -- They walk as ones bound - and they see not for they are as ones blind unto that which I give <u>so</u> <u>freely</u> -- Pity are they which accepts the substitute ---

Pity are they which refuse the real and accept the counterfeit! I say they are pitied ---

Sori Sori -- Be ye as the hand of me the Lord thy God - and come unto this altar this day - as it is expedient for the times of this day - the times of times-- This is most expedient - that this be written as I say it. For this have I prepared thee - and for that matter thou hast learned obedience - and for that do I say: thou art mine hand - even as I am mine Father's -- For it is because of thine preparation that I am able to give unto thee this word ---

Bless thyself to receive it -- So let it be for the good of all -- Amen and Amen ---

Be ye as one on whose shoulders rests the responsibility of this mine house - and it behooves me to say unto thee - it is well - for none other do I find which is prepared to take upon themself such responsibility -- So be it I find them lacking - they are prone to slothfulness and wanton - they fear for nought - they fear that which is nought -- They make mountains of molehills and fall upon them in exhaustion - they do not have the strength to climb them -- Poor in spirit art they - for they have not as yet learned the lesson at hand -- So be it I speak that which I know - that which I see -- So be it that I shall do a marvelous thing - and I shall be unto thee all that ye shall have need of. So let it be - for this have I spoken unto thee thusly - and this mine word shall be placed in the record - as it is given for that purpose - that it might be made part of the record - so shall it be added too -- Let it be said that I am with thee - and I shall sustain thee - with mine rod and mine staff shall ye be sustained ---

Fear nought - walk ye with surety - and I shall delight in thee -- So be it and Selah ---

Be as the mouth of me the Lord thy God - and say unto them that which I would have thee say -- It is come when all their energy shall be spent - and it shall profit them nought -- When it is come that they are called forth from their dwelling place - shall it profit them that which they do? - that which they have done? I say - they shall be as ones empty - and they shall be naked - for they have not fortuned unto them self that which shall profit them -- They have spoken much - they have discoursed much of and about <u>things</u> which are not of me -- They have spoken of ME - yet have they done that which I say? - that which I say,- that which I give unto them to do?-- I say - they are as ones blind and deaf - yet they are as fallow soil - they have not been touched - they are as yet dormant - they produce not -- They are as ones walking blindly.- they stumble in their blindness - and comprehend not that which I say unto them ---

Behold the hand of God move - for I shall make fertile the soil -- I shall bring upon the Earth the rains - and the Sun shall shine - and the winter shall pass - and the spring shall come - bringing forth a bountiful crop - for I say the time is come when the fallow ground shall be broken and it shall bring forth a bountiful harvest ---

Be ye as the hand of me made manifest - and give unto them this mine word - and it shall profit them to heed that which I say -- It is given unto me to see them eating and drinking - singing their merry tunes - playing the games which suit their fancy -- They are fiddling while the city burns about them ---

Now I say - they shall be brot up short - and they shall be caused to become sober -- I say they are reeling to and fro as ones drunken - They are as yet not prepared to take up mine cross and follow where I would lead them -- Now it is come when they shall be as ones which shall pay the fiddler -- They shall see that which is to be done and they shall do it - or they shall move into the place prepared for the laggards ---

They are confused and bewildered - they see not in that which is to do. They speak spurious sayings - and know not the meaning thereof - Let it be said that there is but one Lord God - One Host of Hosts - and I am he - I am HE! Sent that they become aware of that which I AM - and they shall become sobered - they shall walk upright - and with surety -- They shall give nothing unto the dragon which shall comfort him -- They shall be alert - and be as ones watchful - and fortune unto themself the greater part -- So be it and Selah ---

I come that it be SO ---

I dwell within this house and I bid them which enter herein: Be ye thotful of thine Host - for I AM HE which hast founded it - and I have brot it forth in LOVE and LABOR - now ye shall walk gently therein. So let it profit thee -- I am the Lord of Hosts - the Porter at the Gate.

Sori Sori -- Begin the day with thanksgiving and a glad heart - for I say unto thee - great shall be thy harvest -- I say: Be ye as one blest - for by thine own sowing - so shall ye reap -- I say - the ground is prepared and the seeds are within thine own hand -- Go ye forth as one prepared - and bear ye in mind thou art not alone - for I am the "Overseer" - and I shall give unto thee that which is needful and justified - so be it - as ye are prepared so shall ye receive -- So let it profit thee to follow me where I lead thee -- Profit thyself and give not unto the laggards of thine energy - let them not usurp thine strength - thine time-- So be it I shall begin a new work which shall be unto thee great joy -- I say: Behold ye the hand of God - see it move –

Wait upon me the Lord they God ---

Ask of no man his blessing - be ye as one with me -- Bear ye mine name - in the name of Mine Father - for I say unto thee - thou art one with me - and I am one with thee -- Bear ye mine name and know ye that I have given it unto thee in the name of mine Father -- Yet I say unto thee: There are ones which would pilfer the name - and which would give unto thee the bitter cup -- Yet I say unto thee - drink not of the bitter cup - for it is not for thee -- Let them drink of their own poison. Pity them for their foolishness shall rebound upon them -- While I say I give unto thee mine name - I say I have not bestowed upon another - the authority to bear mine name - for I have poured out mine spirit upon thee - and I have authorized thee to speak for me - <u>in mine name</u> - as the one which I have appointed Priestess of this Temple.

And it is given unto me to see them bow before men which do pilfer mine name and mine sayings -- I say unto thee: Bow ye unto NO man for he is but the same yesterday and today - there is but little change -- Man boasts of his wisdom - yet he knows not the law of "Cause and effect" - he waits the day when he shall be prepared - yet he hast fortuned unto himself many days in which to prepare himself - yet he fiddles and dances while all about him proves false - and he wears the skirts of the priest - which avails him nought -- I say the robe hides him not - for I see him as one filled with foul air -- Boast not - be ye as one prepared to go where I lead thee - fear not -- Hear ye me and keep thine eyes open - and put thine hand in mine and ye shall not fall ---

Sori Sori --- Hail! Hail! A prince is come -- Hail! Hail unto the prince - for he is come -- I say a prince is come - and it shall be given unto thee to know him - for he walks the hiways of Earth with ease - and with gentle feet and an humble heart does he pass this way -- Hail! Hail unto the PRINCE - for he comes as the Emissary of the King -- Be ye as one prepared to receive him for he draweth nigh -- Blest are they which receive him and of him - for the wears the royal crown - for he is of the house of Israel - the House of the King of Kings --

Sori Sori -- Hold high thine head and be ye as one blest - for I say unto thee: No greater hast any man than thine inheritance - no greater hast any man ---

So let it be said that I am come that ye receive thine in full - for it is kept intact for thee - and no man shall take from thee one iota - <u>neither</u> shall he add to - for it is complete - complete I say ---

Praise ye the Lord of Hosts - praise ye the Name of Solen Aum Solen -- Call ye unto the Lord of Hosts - and he shall give unto thee that which is expedient - and that which shall be profitable unto them.

Praise ye the Name of Solen Aum Solen - and He shall give unto thee as He hast given unto me -- So be it and Selah --

Hold high the banner of Truth and Justice - and be ye as one which hast been the guardian of Truth and Justice for lo many an age ---

Prepare thineself for to receive thine inheritance in full - for it is intact - even so - so shall ye receive it -- Let it be said that I am the KEEPER of thine inheritance -- And I am a protector - I am the overseer, the guardian - and I guard well - for I am responsible for mine part - and no man shall trip me up -- So be it and Selah ---

I am come that ye be made whole - and that ye be made <u>new</u> -- So be it that I am <u>He</u> which is Sent that it be so - that it be done - that it be accomplished ---

So let it be ---

I am He which is the Guardian of Truth and Justice -- So let it be. Selah and Amen ---

Heed His Counsel!
The Only Way to PEACE!!

Sori Sori -- Be ye as the hand of me and give unto them this mine word and it shall suffice them -- They shall bear witness of mine word - and they shall hold it sacred and they shall be as ones blest to be a part of the plan which now unfolds before them ---

I say they shall be blest! So let it be ---

For this do I give unto them this mine word -- Whatever be done in the world of man is with the intent of man - for man hast been given the law - the mind with which to work -- It is now come when the world of man is in a precarious state - and he hast not the mind to be his own deliverer - his own <u>Savior</u> - for he hast gone far afield -- He hast entangled himself - and now he finds himself entangled in all manner of conditions which are foreign unto him -- He hast not the strength - neither the wisdom to untangle his affairs -- Therefore it behooves me to send into his midst one which shall have the wisdom and power - for he is trained well in the affairs of governments - and these things bother him not - neither shall they confuse him -- So be it that he shall walk with the heads of government - and he shall counsel them - and lead them in the way in which they shall go ---

While many shall turn him away - heeding not his counsel! These shall be as the "Fools" - for I say unto the man of Earth - he shall take heed of mine word and he shall be as one <u>prepared</u> to enter into the great and mighty Council - which is the over all council ---

Now it is for this that the Earth hast been exiled - that She hast been in quarantine - for She hast been a wayward planet - giving footing to many generations of rebels - "Rebels" I say -- These rebels have rebelled against the law - the WORD OF GOD - and they have been as the "Prodigal Son" -- I say: They have rebelled against the High and Mighty Council - for they have not accepted that which hast been set before them -- They speak of <u>Peace</u>! Peace? - wherein is "Peace" to be found <u>in</u> <u>them</u>? I say: Let "Peace" be established within thine heart - and <u>no</u> <u>man</u> shall take it from thee!

Bear ye in mind - I am come that it be established amongst men - that it be established within the <u>heart</u> of men ---

PEACE? Wherein is it written that peace shall reign within thine heart? ---

I say: Be ye as one at peace - and ye shall be as one with ME ---

Let it be said this day - I am not alone - I bring with me a mighty host - a number of <u>warriors</u> - well trained in the affairs of governments. They are well qualified to meet all the situations which confront men of Earth ---

Now I say again - that one shall be sent into all the chambers wherein sit the high and mighty Counselors of the law - and he shall do a mighty work -- Yet the time is not <u>yet</u> come when each and every one shall pay heed unto his counsel -- Be ye ever mindful of these mine words - and let not <u>thine</u> foot slip -- Pay ye heed unto that which I have said -- Feign not <u>wisdom</u> - for thou art amongst the unknowing which hast been enmeshed within the tangled web which now threatens to engulf thy civilization - and destroy it completely - <u>forever!</u> So I say unto thee: Be ye as one patient - and love thine neighbor as thyself -- Call no man a fool until thou hast proven thine own wisdom -- Wash thine own hands - before thou callest his dirty -- Bless thyself by the cleansing -- Be ye as one thotful of mine word - mine work - mine Counsel - and I shall take thot of thee -- So be it I have spoken - and pray thou hearest ME ---

Sori Sori -- This day I would say unto thee: Be ye as one blest - and say unto them which come unto thee - there is but little time in which to prepare - for it is given unto man to be without the light which is his salvation - without hope - without the assistance of the Great and Mighty Council -- I say - it is given unto me to know the part which man hast portioned out for himself - and he hast portioned out a bitter portion -- Yet he shall stand as one responsible for his part -- He hast fostered a race of bastards - and a people which hast not heeded the word -- He hast given of himself unto the forces of darkness -- He hast followed blindly the ones which know not the way -- I say they too are lost - for they have not followed in mine footsteps -- I am come that they have light - and that they be brot out of their bondage -- While I am not alone in this - I say - many walk in flesh as thou - yet they are prone to spurn the help which we would give unto them - yet I say unto them - by their fruit ye shall know them -- They boast not - neither do they claim great and grand rewards of men -- They ask nought - for I say unto them - the way of the Lord is made strait before thee - and I the Lord thy God bid thee enter therein with surety and ye shall not be misled - for I come as a thief in the night - and I bid thee look! Watch! and see - for I am come that ye might know the TRUTH - and no man shall deny thee --

SEEK ME - THE LIGHT -- Ask no man his opinion - and be ye as one prepared to go where I lead thee -- Praise ye the Father which hast Sent ME - and He shall be unto thee ALL that ye have need of --

So be it and Selah ---

Sori Sori -- Blest be this day -- Blest be this day -- Blest be this day. Let this day bring forth a new order - and let it be done with the joy which comes with obedience unto the law -- I am come that a new order might be brot forth - established upon the Earth -- I come not to destroy the law - but to establish it - to confirm the law - to finish that which I began so long ago -- For mine work wast not finished on Calvary -- Mine work is not finished now - yet I come that it be brot forth that which is to be -- For it is given unto me to be as one present at this moment -- I am not confined to a body of flesh - for I have overcome flesh -- Flesh no longer binds me - I go and come at will - I need no bed in which to rest mine form ---

Form? Yea - I am form - I have form - I am the Master of form -- I can take upon myself any form for the work which I choose to do -- I am not limited to size or color - neither the form or garments I wear -- Space - nor time bothers me not - for I am the one which hast been freed of all bondage -- Now I come that ye might be free even as I - that ye might go where I go -- I say: Place thine hand in mine and I shall lead thee -- Fortune thyself the better part - follow ye me -- Weep not for them which put their foot against me - for I say unto thee: They shall be as ones responsible for their foolishness ---

Resist them not -- Pray that they see the folly of their ways -- Bless thyself by thine own prayers for them - for hatred is but a thorn in thine own heel ---

Sori Sori -- Hold high the torch which I give unto thee -- Bear in mind that which I say unto thee - and walk ye with dignity -- Bear ye the toth which I place upon thee - for none shall soil it - neither shall they take from thee thine inheritance -- None shall be unto thee thine salvation - for I have given unto thee passport into the place of mine abode -- I say unto thee "Pass" - let it be -- As thou hast prepared thyself I say: "Pass ye in" -- So be it I know thee - and no man shall say thee nay ---

Be ye as one blest this day for I am with thee ---

Behold ye the work which I do - behold ye that which I do - for I say unto thee: I am alert unto the needs of mine servants - and they shall not want - I say: "THEY WHICH SERVE ME SHALL NOT WANT".

Too - I say:

They which serve me with one hand and mammon with the other - is but a foolish servant - for it <u>profits</u> him nought ---

For I ask of him himself - a living sacrifice - which I might use that mine Father be glorified -- So be it that I have spoken - let it be as it is spoken -- Bear ye in mind - I ask nought save obedience unto the law:- as thou art prepared so shall ye receive -- So be it and Selah ---

Sori Sori -- Sananda is the Lord God of the Realm -- and he is thy doorkeeper - thine Guardian thru which ye shall enter into the Realm of Light wherein ALL things are known -- Be ye not weary - for I say unto thee: Thy time cometh when ye shall walk the byways of the Celestial Realms with surety -- Ye shall know that which I Know - ye shall be as one which hast overcome all <u>things</u> - and ye shall walk in freedom - even as I -- Prepare thyself - for I say: Thy time cometh - and ye shall hear the word: "Well done" and ye shall be glad ---

By the hand of the Almighty God which is ABOVE ALL shall ye receive thine full inheritance - and ye shall know thyself to be one with Him which is over All -- So be it that I say unto thee: "Be ye as one prepared to enter therein"---

Hold high thy head - bear thy cross with dignity - and be ye not anxious - for I say: <u>Thy</u> <u>time</u> cometh -- Wherein is it said that it shall be given unto thee to go the way in which I go -- Ye shall go all the way with me -- Ye shall not fail - ye SHALL be the Victor -- So be it and Selah ---

Bother not with the <u>opinions</u> of men - ask of them no favors - forch not thine learning upon them - bear ye in mind they too are fortuned the law - they too are given the law -- They have been brot forth that they might finish their part -- Let it be said that which I have said before: Many are called - few are chosen - for they have not accepted that which I have for them - they have chosen the lesser part -- So be it as they are prepared so shall they receive ---

Sori Sori -- For this day would I speak unto thee -- For this time I would say: Be ye mine hand - and give unto them this mine word - and it shall profit them to receive it unto themself --For there is but little time left for that which is to be done -- I say - little time is left - for the Age past hast not produced that which is Light -- Darkness is over the land - the people in bondage - and the land encompassed on every side by enemies - and the land is desecrated by mans ignorance -- I am come this day that the darkness be dispelled - and that the way be made strait.

Be it the Father's Will that I come bearing with me a <u>Mighty</u> <u>Host</u> - which shall go forth as ones prepared -- I say they shall go forth as to battle - and they shall not fail - neither shall they want ---

Forget not that the Earth and the fullness thereof is His - while the darkness is of man's creation -- Man creates his confusion and torment. I say he IS tormented! So shall he turn from his own creation - and seek the Light which I AM ---

Be ye as one prepared to walk the Royal Road -- Be ye as one which hast mine hand on thine - and I shall lead thee -- I shall give unto thee as thou art prepared to receive -- Let it be known that which I say - for it is given unto them which are prepared to receive -- I am come that they might know me - and that they be prepared to receive as I have received of Mine Father-- So be it and Selah ---

Fortune thyself the Greater part - for it is thine inheritance <u>in</u> <u>full.</u> -

Bless thyself -- Bless thyself -- Bless thyself --

Sori Sori -- This day I would speak unto thee of one which is to come -- It is mine part to send one into thine midst - and he shall be as one prepared to give unto thee as he hast received of me - for this is he sent -- He shall be as one with me - he shall stand as one <u>with</u> <u>me</u> - he shall be qualified to do mine work for he is well trained -- I have prepared him well - for he hast given of himself that he might be as a fit servant in mine house ---

Now ye shall be as one prepared to receive him -- He shall know that which is to do - and he shall be about the business at hand - and no man shall distract him or stumble him -- Bless thyself to receive him. He cometh from afar - and he holds within his hand the Key to the inner temple -- Ye shall know him and ye shall accept him for that which he is -- So be it and Selah ---

Sori Sori -- Wherein is it said that there shall be great stress upon the peoples of the Earth ---

It is now come and it shall be as it is written -- Yet it is said: "One shall come which shall be unto the nations great light"-- He shall bring with him great knowledge and strength -- Wisdom shall be his - and he shall walk with the heads of all governments - and he shall counsel them as they have <u>not</u> been counseled aforetime ---

While it is said: He shall counsel them - it too is said that not all shall heed his counsel -- Therefore it behooves me to give unto them this word: They shall be given the word - and they shall be forewarned. When they reject it they shall bear witness of their folly - for <u>they shall see</u> the folly of their way -- They shall bear the responsibility of their folly!---

Now it is come when many shall be brot out aforehand - and they shall know no suffering - while others shall find themself trapt within the web -- It is not willed thus by the Mighty Council -- Wherein is it said: Bring thyself as a living sacrifice unto the altar of the Most High Living God -- Wherein hast it been said that they which surrender up themself shall find me - therein is much to ponder -- Hast it not been said: "Follow me - come as a <u>living</u> sacrifice and I shall bring thee out of bondage" ---

I say unto them: "Flesh shall not bind thee - flesh shall be unto thee as nought - for ye shall overcome flesh"---

Bring thyself as a LIVING SACRIFICE - surrender up thyself that I might use thee for to glorify the Father which is not flesh!

HE IS NOT FLESH!

Be ye even as HE!

Be ye free from all which binds thee -- Walk ye the Royal Road - and rejoice with me ---

Bear ye witness of Me -

Break Bread with Me -

Eat - and hunger no more -

Be ye as one blest -

Amen and Selah ---

Moreover I say unto thee: Write this which I say unto thee - that it may go into the record - for it shall profit them which shall come after thee ---

There shall be one sent into thy midst - and he shall take upon himself the task of bringing order out of chaos - and he shall be as one prepared -- He shall wear a garment liken unto man - yet he shall have the wisdom which is not of Earth - for he hast been trained without the Earth - He hast been prepared in a School far removed from the Earth and wherein is peace -- I say: "He hast been prepared in a school FAR removed from the Earth - wherein there is Peace!" ---

Now he comes swiftly and with surety -- He shall walk - and counsel - and direct the ones which are prepared to receive him and of him ---

He hast waited for the time which is now come -- So be it and Selah. Give ye thanks it is come - for it is a day of rejoicing ---

Hold ye high the banner which I give unto thee - and ye shall be as one prepared to receive him -- He shall direct thee and lead thee into new fields of endeavor which shall be the way of PEACE! ---

I say unto thee: BEAR YE WITNESS OF ME -- Bear ye witness of MINE WORD - that they might become aware of me -- So be it and Selah ---

BE YE THE WITNESS ---

The Peace Maker

Sori Sori -- Mine hand is swift and sure - and I shall place it upon thee in Holy benediction -- And for this shall ye be as one prepared for the part which is now prepared for thee -- Ye shall be as one on which I have poured out mine Spirit - and for this shall ye receive that which I have for thee -- I say it shall be the beginning of a new part - and none shall reject it - which are <u>prepared</u> to receive me ---

I come unto thee this morning even as of yesterday that ye might have the WORD which shall profit them which are to follow after thee.

The Word shall be Holy - and Pure -- No adulteration shall enter therein - for I say unto thee that which I will - for I Know that which I am about - that which is well to say ---

There be ones which reject this mine word - for it is not unto their liking - they would have great phrases and flowery words denoting their way - the way of the <u>priest</u> - yet I say I come not as they are wont - I come that they be free from their bondage - their opinions and conceit.- I say - I come that they be free from all their fetishes - all their dogmas. Wherein hast it profited them? ---

Now I say: I come as the Counselor - the lawyer - the older brother, the one Sent of mine Father that His Will be done ---

The trickery - the conceit - the mockery of men matters NOT to ME. Yet I say - it is their <u>lot</u> - their own misdeeds - their own obligation to bring themself unto the altar of the Most High <u>Living</u> <u>God</u> - clean and pure ---

They shall turn from their puny ways - of conceit/ deceit/ anger/ hatred/ and for that matter slaughter - yea - that which is not of ME ---

Then I shall lay hands upon them - and I shall bless them as I have been blest -- Then they shall have passport into the place of mine abode.

Yea - into the "Inner Temple" wherein ALL things are known ---

I come that it be so - so let it be - as the Father hast willed it ---

Bear ye in mind I am come that there be LIGHT - for I Am the Light - I Am the Light - I AM THE LIGHT -- I am He which is come to bear witness of mine Father -- So be it He and I are One -- For this am I prepared to do His WILL -- So be it I ask of thee obedience unto the law -- I give it unto thee as it is given unto me -- It is the same yesterday and today ---

I say the <u>law</u> of which I teach is the same yesterday and today -- While the law of Earth differs from the law of another realm - the law of which I speak differs not in any realm - it holds within all realms - it varies not ---

While the governments of men differ one from the other - the government of the Great and Mighty Council - the <u>Over-All</u> Council holds good - varying not in and over all governments - be they of what-so-ever realm---

The Law of Love and compassion is not the governing force of Earth-man - for he heeds not that which is said unto them -- He - for the most part makes a mockery of that which hast been written as "Law"-- They are want to belittle the LAW which is given - which would bind all men together in One common bond of love -- Wherein is it said - they are prone to hatred and war - they are prone to murder and sacrifice the blood of the innocent -- I say - they are the "Sacrificers" - they are not the ones which have brot "Peace" -- "Peace" is not yet established within their hearts - they are not the "Peace Makers" ---

Yet I have said: A "Peace maker" shall walk in their midst - and they shall be afrighted - for he shall be at peace amongst them -- They shall be as ones fearful within his presence - for they shall stand as ones ashamed - and as ones shorn of their glory -- They shall be as naked before him - they shall fall down and cry for mercy - and they shall speak words of love and they shall turn to follow him -- These shall be brot out - and they shall be as ones blest of him - for they shall be as ones prepared for greater things -- So be it and Selah ---

Sori Sori -- Hast it not been said that one shall come into thy midst for to lift thee up?- and it is so -- So be it that he shall wear the Crown of Victory - for he hast overcome flesh and the perils thereof --So be it that he shall go and come at will - for he hast won his freedom -- He no longer is bound by the bonds of Earth - he shall be as free - FREE I say! He shall be as one free to go and come at will ---

While he shall appear as flesh - I say it is for this that he shall be unto the nations Counselor -- He shall counsel them as men - and unto them he shall come as man - - let it be - - for they comprehend not that which they see not ---

While that which they see not is of Greater power than that which they see - I say - they see not the REAL but the shadow - the part which is the denser -- They see not that which passes not away - they fear that which they see not -- Yet they see not beyond their flesh or material world -- Therefore - I say unto thee: Look - behold! that which shall be made manifest before thee -- Yet it shall be the unseen which shall be made seen -- That which shall be made seen shall be that which they I have not seen - for it shall come to pass that the unseen shall become seen - and they shall be as ones affrighted - and they shall cry out - for they have not prepared themself for this day - when great things shall be revealed unto them ---

They shall bear witness of this mine word - for I shall do a wondrous work - and they shall bear testimony of the thing which I shall do -- So be it and Selah ---

Sori Sori -- I have this day decreed for thee the way which ye shall go - and ye shall no more wander in darkness - for I say unto thee: Thy time hast come when ye shall be enlightened - ye shall be ENLIGHTENED - and no more shall ye walk in darkness - for it shall come to pass that ye shall surmount the darkness - and ye shall <u>walk</u> in the Light! ---

I say: Ye shall walk knowingly and ye shall be glad for thy knowing. Let thine light so shine that it be seen from afar - and ye shall not put thine light under a cover that it be seen not ---

Rest ye in the KNOWING that I have decreed for thee that which is to be -- So let it be -- Wait upon me the Lord God - the Host of Hosts, the Light which faileth not ---

Bless them which come unto thee -- Let them see that which they have eyes to see - and be ye not weary of their foolishness - for they too have a part -- As they prepare themself - so shall they receive - so let it be -- For this I say unto thee: "Prepare thyself for greater things".

So let them seek the Light which I Am ---

Preparedness

Sori Sori Let this begin a new part - and let it be called the part which is Preparedness -- And it shall be for the ones which are prepared for the "Greater Part" -- These which are prepared shall find that they have prepared themself for to receive me and of me - for they shall be as the ones which have complied with the law -- They shall be as the ones which have served me lovingly and with devotion to truth and justice. And it is given unto them to walk gently amongst their fellow men -- They walk with humility and with dignity - asking no favors - accepting no favors -- They are not prone unto flattery -- They fear no evil -- They boast not - neither do they want -- They are quiet - and they keep a civil tongue -- They weary not of men of less stature - they see them as they are -- They are want to assist the ones of lesser stature -- While they <u>are not</u> the porters - they stand ready to assist when and where it is necessary and wise to do so ---

They are as ones aware of that which goes on about them - yet they <u>fear</u> <u>not</u> - for they know wherein they are staid --They know they are part of the <u>Great</u> and <u>Grand</u> <u>Plan</u> -- They do that which is given unto them to do - and they weary not of that which is given unto them - they see and know that there is a <u>Divine</u> <u>Plan</u> - and it is given unto them to be obedient unto the law which governs the Plan --

They are as ones which have followed the way set before them -- They walk in the way set before them - they are as ones prepared to go all the way with me. They know me for that which I Am - and they ask not where I Am - neither do they seek me afar -- They KNOW ME and where to find me for it is said: "As ye are prepared so shall ye receive"- and as they prepare themself so shall I shew myself unto them --

And they shall be as ones which know that I Am - that I Am he which comes and which goes at will -- I tarry not in <u>one</u> <u>place</u> - yet I am not excluded at any time from any place -- No lock - no door bars my way - it is not necessary that I have invitations - yet when I am the welcome Visitor I know how to approach - I make known myself at the time most appropriate - for <u>I</u> Know the appropriate time ---

I am not asleep - I am alert unto that which goes on - and I need no books/ radios/ neither thy puny news media - for I have the Greater Vision which fails not ---

I say: There is wisdom in mine words - be ye thotful of them - and know ye that I am that which I Am - and I shall do that which I say I will to do -- And none shall make VOID mine word -- So be it that I have not bungled the words which I have given herein -- I am not unlearned in these things -- I am the Master of languages - and I know the "Ethic" of thine schools -- I see them for that which they are -- Yet

I do not see them as places of LEARNING - they are prone to be the lesser places of learning - for I say: I have Schools of Greater Learning which they are not qualified to enter --

Therefore I say unto thee my readers: Be ye not hasty to criticize my part/ my method of teaching -- Be ye as one content to learn that which I have to teach thee -- I break no law - neither do I break mine word---

I keep my word - I keep mine Covenant with Mine Father which hast Sent Me ---

So be ye as one prepared for that which I have for thee ---

The Path

= Ye Shall =

Sori Sori This would I say unto them which are prepared to receive of me: "Ye shall know wherein ye are staid - and ye shall be unafraid - for ye shall know that I Am with thee"-- Ye shall be as the "Rock" -- Ye shall be as one which hast thy hand in mine - and ye shall go where I lead thee -- Ye shall be "On the Path" and ye shall know it to be TRUTH for ye shall be firm in thy convictions -- Ye shall waver not -- Ye shall be as one which can see that which goes on about thee without fear or hatred -- Ye shall be as the one which knows the way - and ye shall walk in it without fear or doubt ---

= Be Ye =

Be ye strong in thy convictions --

Be ye staunch in thy faith --

Be ye as one responsible for thy convictions --

Be ye as one which hast given of thyself that ye may know the truth.

Be ye merciful and just - yet ye shall make no alliance with the forces of darkness --

Be ye as a BEACON set on a hill - that <u>they</u> might see it and be drawn unto it --

Be ye faithful in thy trust --

Be ye trust worth --

Be ye as the hand of me made manifest --

Be ye prepared to go all the way with me --

Be ye praise worth - yet seeking not favor of men --

Be ye as one which hast the mark of the Lord upon thee - and He shall find thee --

Be ye as one which can hear MINE VOICE - and Know it to be TRUTH --

Be ye as one which hast no enemies - yet keep thine hand on the plow - thine eye on the furrow --

Be ye as one which can give - asking nought --

Be ye as one which can speak without noise --

Be ye as one which can hear without emotion - without anxiety --

Be ye as one which can receive without giving -- Let it be for thy own sake that ye learn the heart of receiving while not giving --

Be ye as one which knows the <u>art</u> of giving while NOT receiving - yet ye shall not be as one confused by this mine word - for I say unto thee: Ye shall not reject mine word - for the reason thou art poor/ for any reason!

Be ye as one understanding - and ye shall be filled with great joy. Be ye as one which can stand in great turmoil undisturbed/ unafraid - while the world trembles -- Be ye at PEACE -- Blest is he which knows Peace - for it is established within him ---

Fortune of Them Which are Prepared

Sori Sori -- Be ye as one blest this day - and know ye that I am with thee - that I am one which hast prepared thee for this part -- And ye shall call this part: the "Fortune of them which are prepared"---

I say unto thee: "The Fortune of them which are prepared is greater than all others"- for they shall receive of The Father even as I have received -- So be it and Selah ---

Be ye as the hand of me made manifest - and record this mine word unto them - for have I not ordained thee mine priestess - and given unto thee the authority to speak in mine name -- Such is the power and authority of mine priestess - for it is now come when greater things shall be done -- And for this have I spoken with thee - and I have counseled thee in the way of the wise - and ye shall stand with me upon mine High Holy Mount as one knowing -- So be it and Selah ---

Fortune thyself the part of messenger and priestess - for this is the work at hand - and it shall profit them which are witnesses of this word and this work shall neither perish nor be forgotten -- For I say I have set up this Altar - and I shall give unto it Life and supply it with Living Water - and it shall not run dry -- So be it I have spoken and it is so decreed that thou hast heard me -- And all which hear shall be glad - for they shall know that which they have heard - and they shall be as ones prepared to go all the way with me ---

These I shall lead into the SECRET PLACE of my abode - wherein they have not been - and they shall find therein a fortune which they have forfeited in ages past-- They shall find therein the wealth which is theirs by Divine inheritance - when they are prepared to receive it ---

They shall find therein the inheritance which they have prepared themself for to receive -- They shall accept it is the name of the Most High God Solen Aum Solen and they shall be free from all shame and guilt/ all fetters - for they shall be as ones clothed in "Pure linen"- and their hands shall be clean -- They shall *be* guiltless and they shall be found trust worth - and no hatred shall be found within them -- For this shall they be found worthy to receive of their heritage ---

Blest shall be these which come into the place wherein I abide - for they SHALL Know God ---

Sori Sori hast it not been given unto thee to walk with me? And hast it not been given unto thee to know me? And hast it not been given unto thee to receive of me thine Authority and thy name? Hast it not been given unto me to come unto thee as flesh made seen - and hast thou not proffered ME bread - while the others saw me not for that which I was/ AM -- I say I am come that ye be brot out of bondage - that ye have thine inheritance---

I come declaring I Am the Truth and the Light - yet did they accept ME? ---

I say they soon forgot that which I gave unto them ---

The ones which followed chose to change the WORD - to take from/ add to - and adulterate the Word which I taught - which I brot unto them from the REALM OF LIGHT - beyond their knowing or remembrance ---

Now as before - I give of mineself that they might be lifted up - that they might come into the <u>fullness</u> of their inheritance -- Yet few are prepared to go where I go ---

Blest are they which are so prepared ---

Blest indeed are they - for they <u>shall</u> see God The Father ---

So be it and Selah ---

Sori Sori -- Be ye as the hand of me made manifest unto them which have eyes to see - ears to hear - and let them <u>see</u> and hear -- For I say unto them: The time is come when I shall make mineself heard and seen for I shall reveal mineself unto them which seek truth and Light -- So be it I am come that they be enlightened -- So let it be ---

I say: They shall be en-Lightened - and they shall walk with me in Light -- So be it that I have poured out mine Spirit on thee - and now ye shall be as one on whose shoulders I place mine mantle -- I shall give unto thee the authority and the power to speak in mine name - and I shall give unto thee the WORD - and it shall not be adulterated in any form - any manner what-so-ever - for I am giving unto thee that which is wise and prudent -- Yet ye shall remember that I have given unto thee thy part separate and apart - that ye be prepared to do this mine work -- I have prepared thee aforehand - and I am prepared to give unto thee in greater measure -- So be it and Selah -- Bear ye in mind - I am he which is come that ALL men be lifted up -- So shall it be -- Yet I have said I shall not tarry with man always -- I shall go - and yet another shall come -- While I say - This is the day of Salvation - I say it is not the end - - - it is not the end of man's work - neither his preparation - for the GREATER PART -- So be it I am HE which is Sent of MINE FATHER that he be delivered out of bondage ---

Sori Sori -- Hold ye fast and be ye as one responsible for thine own part - and let it suffice that I Am with thee -- Yet ye shall be as one with me - and ye shall not fail - neither shall ye want -- Be ye as one prepared for that which is to do or be done -- Behold ye the Hand of God -- See It Move ---

Sori Sori -- Be ye as the hand of me - and give unto them this Mine Word - and it shall profit them to heed that which I say unto them ---

There is one amongst them which hast the power and the authority to give unto them the Water of Life - and they shall be as ones prepared to receive it - for <u>none</u> other receive -- It is NOW come when HE shall walk in their midst and HE shall be as one prepared to bear witness of The Father Which hast Sent <u>ME</u> -- So be it and Selah ---

Be ye as one prepared to receive of HIM - as HE hast received of The Father ---

I say unto thee: Prepare thyself for the fullness of thy estate - for it is thine by Divine inheritance - and none shall enlarge upon it or take from it one iota ---

I say: "<u>None</u> shall enlarge upon it or take from it one iota" -- Be ye as one blest by The Word - and I shall touch thee - and ye shall raise up as on wings - and ye shall no longer be bound by the law of Earth -- Flesh shall no longer bind thee - neither shall ye be bound by anything - <u>neither</u> <u>in</u> <u>Heaven</u> <u>or</u> <u>Earth</u> - for ye shall be unbound ---

By Mine Own Hand shall I unbind thee -- Ye shall be as a Son of God - and ye shall know as <u>I</u> know -- So <u>let</u> it be ---

For this do I say: "Prepare thyself for to receive as <u>I</u> have received of MINE FATHER"-- So be it ye shall be glad for the preparation -- So be it and Selah ---

I say unto thee: Make ready thyself for to receive of the Water of Life - for it shall be proffered unto them which have so prepared themself -- It is given unto me to shew thee the way -- <u>This</u> is the Way of PREPAREDNESS - and it is clearly stated that ye shall do thy part and I shall do mine ---

When thou hast so prepared thyself for to receive me - I shall come unto thee and give unto thee as thou art prepared to receive -- So be it and Selah ---

Bear in mind that I am Sent of Mine Father that ye be eliberated - and that ye be lifted up - that ye be forever <u>one</u> with Him --

I am the DOOR thru which ye enter in --

I am as the fullness of HIS WILL --

I am the Will of Mine Father <u>made</u> <u>manifest</u> ---

I Am His Will - made in His likeness and in His image --

I Am - the Love of The Father made manifest --

I Am He - which hast triumphed over flesh --

I Am He - which hast declared unto thee the law of <u>The</u> <u>One</u> --

I Am HE - which hast revealed unto thee the power of LOVE --

I Am He - which hast given unto thee of Mineself that ye be made perfect in Him - So be it and Selah ---

I Am He - which hast walked with thee in the of time of stress --

I Am He - which hast preserved thee for this day-- So be it that I Am - come this day that ye might be like unto Him Which hast Sent Me -- I Am He - which now stands upon the "High Holy Mount" and bids thee follow <u>Me</u> - for I shall lead thee into the place wherein <u>all</u> things are known -- So <u>let</u> it be ---

Praise ye the Name of Solen Aum Solen - for HE alone is the CAUSE of thy BEING ---

So be it that ye shall receive of Him thine heritage - and no more shall ye be found wanting/ no more shall ye be bound in flesh ---

I say: HAIL! Hail!- unto The Victor!

Hail Hail - O ye Son of the MOST HIGH LIVING GOD - Hail! thou - MIGHTY SON!

Arise! Arise! All ye children of Earth - and be ye as ones prepared to receive as <u>I</u> have <u>received</u> - and there shall be great joy thruout All the COSMOS ---

Be ye as ones alert - for I say unto THEE: This is the day of <u>DECISION</u> - and ye shall choose thy course - and I say unto <u>THEE</u>: Thine choice shall be thine own - for none shall bring thee against thy will -- So be it I <u>bid</u> thee come - yet I shall not bring thee against thy will ---

I say: Behold - the Glory of The Lord Thy God - and I say unto thee: LOOK! SEE! and thou hast put thine hand before thine eyes that ye see not -- And thou hast turned thine face from Me - and set thine foot against Me -- NOW I say: Look - See - and thou shall bless thyself to look - to see - to heed - to follow where I Lead thee ---

Be blest this day - and I shall shew thee many things which thou hast not seen - neither hast thou dreamed of that which I have to shew thee ---

Fortune thyself such as I have kept for thee -- Be ye forever blest. So <u>let</u> it be ---

I Am Sananda --

Sori Sori -- Mine beloved: Mine hand is upon thee and ye shall be reminded of ME - for I shall do that which I have said I shall do - and ye shall know that I have fulfilled mine part with thee ---

Now ye shall be as one alert - and ye shall be as one prepared for a new part - the next part - and it shall be for them which are prepared to receive it-- So be it as they are prepared ---

Fortune <u>thyself</u> to be prepared -- While many ask concerning their preparation - I say: They are <u>to</u> <u>be</u> as ones prepared for the Greater Part for it is now come when the world-of-man shall be shaken unto the very foundation!

It shall quake and fall - and upon <u>The</u> <u>Rock</u> shall be built the <u>NEW</u> foundation - for the one which is now in decay shall be removed unto the last vistage - and a new and firm foundation shall be laid - for to receive the next generation -- While I say it shall be prepared for the next generation - I too say - that the next Generation shall find a Great Change - and much to do to bring about the favorable conditions in which the work of the "New Age" of Light might be done -- I say: They shall have a Great <u>responsibility</u> - for they shall be as the ones responsible for <u>their</u> <u>part</u> - which shall be to finish that which hast NOW been commenced -- I say they shall be as ones to finish that which is now obvious unto thee ---

Thou seest something afar - yet ye see not clearly that which is being done -- And thou lookest hither and yon for signs of the "New Order" - yet it appears at this moment to be chaos ---

While it is said: "Thou lookest hither and yon"- it is said that ye shall see that which goes on about thee -- Ye shall be as one which hast eyes to see - and a mind to learn - for it is plain unto thee that changes are being made - and many are inquiring: "Where Whither - When - Why Lord???

Many are fearful - many anxious - many are faint and sick - hungry and dying - without the knowledge of me - without the comfort of hope yet I am near unto them -- So be it that I am not of a mind to forsake them which have a mind to receive me -- I shall lift them up and give unto them that which they are prepared to receive -- So be it and Selah.

Bear ye in mind that the body is but the flesh which shall not endure it shall return unto the elements from whence it came -- While the Spirit of man shall endure - and it shall arise as the Eagle - the Victor - and it shall be Victor over the animal body - which shall no more bind the ones which are prepared to receive of me - and by ME -- I say: They shall ARISE as on wings - and be as ones free forevermore -- So be it that I have said so -- I have declared unto thee the WORD -- So shall it be -- Let it be as I have spoken -- So shall the Word be fulfilled according unto the Will of Mine Father which hast Sent ME ---

Sori Sori -- Hear ye me and be ye as one which hast mine hand upon thee - and give unto them this Mine Word - that they might know that which I say -- I am the Lord God - the fortune of the Earth and Heaven. I Know that which I am about - and I am not deceived by the cry of Lord! Lord! I am not moved by their pious prayers and repetitious sayings - "their" decrees -- I am not moved by their pain - I am moved to bring about their deliverance!!

I am moved to give unto them the law - that they might know the LAW - that they might fulfill it - that they might be forever free from bondage ---

I say unto thee: I am come into their midst that they might know the true from the false -- So be it and Selah ---

I say: They cry for surcease from pain - and too I say - they cry for freedom from bondage - yet they know not wherein they are bound -- I say unto thee: "I Am Come that they be <u>forever</u> free"-- So be it and Selah ---

I am the Author and the finisher of this Mine work - and I shall not give unto them the bitter cup -- Yet I say: They shall drink of the cup which they prepare for <u>themself</u> - for I am not the one which prepares it for them - it is of their own making -- So let them drink of their own cup -- While I say COME - they deny me - they hear not - they spit on mine servants - and they give of their time unto the dragon and his will.

I say: They serve the dragon willing or unwilling -- He hast prepared many a snare for them - that he entrap them -- So be it that I say: Turn from him - and be ye as one prepared to go where I go - Hasten ye - that ye might be brot out before it is too late---

So be it I have spoken -- So shall I speak again and again ---

Sori Sori -- So be it that there is one amongst thee which hast the mark of the beast upon him - and he hast a seat in high places - and he shall do a thing which shall be unto him his undoing -- He shall be his own judge - and his own accuser - and he shall be overthrown - for he shall overstep his authority -- Let it be said - it is so ordained - for he is in the place wherein he hast sat but a short while - for a purpose yet unknown to the populace -- Now it is come when many things shall be brot to light - that the populace might be enlightened - unto the perils which the country faces -- I say: It (U.S.A.) faces great danger -- So be it I would have it enlightened - therefore I shall do that which I will ---

Be ye as ones alert - and give unto <u>Me</u> credit for Knowing that which goes on in the world-of-men ---

I say: It is now come when one shall walk within thy midst - which shall find them which are prepared to follow me - and I say - I shall do a marvelous work - for I shall set up a Kingdom which shall be unlike that which <u>shall be</u> overthrown - and it shall endure - for it shall be built upon a Solid Foundation --

For this have I set Mine Seal upon them which have come out from among them which serve "mammon" -- I say the temples of the money lenders shall be overthrown - and they shall be brot low -- So be it I have spoken - and I am speaking out - on behalf of mine children which are sorely oppressed!

So shall I continue to persue the law of Justice and Peace - yet I say I bring with me a legion of warriors - which carry no weapons save the Sword of Truth and Justice - for this is the weapon of power - which is given unto the soldiers of Light - which have learned well the futility of war -- I say - they have learned the futility of "war" - the way of the aggressor - the futility of hatred and oppression --

They have come from the legions of Earth in times past - they have been well schooled in the realms of Light - wherein they have seen the records of Earth and Her peoples -- For long have they studied these records - and found that the way of Eternal Peace is Love - and by no other plan shall Peace be found ---

So be it that I now sit upon the right hand of Mine Father - and I declare unto thee: There is a <u>plan</u> - a Divine Plan whereby man shall be delivered out of his bondage ---

Yet I say: He first shall lay down his arms - and take up <u>his</u> cross and follow ME - and I shall give unto him that which I have kept for him for THIS DAY -- So be it that I have announced Mine intentions - and that I shall do -- So be it and Selah ---

I am the Lord God - and I speak with the Authority envested in Me of Mine Father Which hast Sent Me -- So be it and Selah ---

Be ye not anxious - for I am with thee unto the end -- Fortune thyself that which I have for thee --

Discernment

Be ye as one on whose shoulders I place Mine mantle - and I say unto thee: I am the Lord God - Sent of Mine Father that ALL men be lifted up -- Therefore I say unto them: "Lift up thine feet and come" - Come out from amongst the people which hast portioned out the poison for themself -- Hear ye Me - and bring thyself out from amongst them which violate the law -- I say: Ye shall dare be different - and ye shall walk in the Way I lead thee --

Ye shall fear not the scorn of man - neither shall ye fear the wrath of men - their weapons - nor the pity of their plight -- And the words of their mouth shall fall upon thine ears as a breeze - blown by a gentle wind -- Ye shall not heed that which they say - ye shall follow after Me the Lord thy God - and I shall lead thee out of the pit - and ye shall not fail---

No man shall drag thee down - for I shall sustain thee in all thine ways -- Ye shall <u>Know</u> the Truth and it shall set thee free -- So be it and Selah -- Mine Word is sacred and Holy - and no man shall invalidate it -- No man shall set his hand unto Mine Mouth - for I shall say that which is needful and expedient ---

I shall put Mine foot against the door wherein the profane would rush in -- I shall put asunder the works of the wicked - and it shall be as ash beneath the feet of the RIGHTEOUS - for I shall not surrender up Mine People -- I shall not fail thee in thine trial and in thine time of want - for I am a just and righteous man - which hast gone before thee and I know whereof I speak - and I am prepared to go all the way with thee -- Bear ye witness of Me - walk with Me - and know ye that I am with thee --

Be ye not deceived by their garments - and pretty speeches for I say: They come in a variety of costumes - claiming to be "HE" - and they know not that they blaspheme the Name of the One in Whose Name I come -- I say - they know not the Name of Solen Aum Solen - they know not that which they do - for they are want to storm the gate yet I say: I Am the Porter at the Gate and I know them ---

Let them first learn the way of Righteousness - and then they shall walk in the way I set before them - and then they shall walk gently and be at peace - they shall KNOW PEACE -- Be it so - and so be it -- For this do I speak unto thee - that <u>they</u> might know that which I say -- Let it be well with thee - for I am with thee unto the end ---

Recorded by Sister Thedra

Say unto them: The Word of God shall be as a two edged Sword -- It shall cut away all that which hast bound them - and that which hast held them in bondage - lo the eons - and it shall bring to light that which hast been hidden -- While I say - it shall cut away all that hast bound them it shall free them - and they shall be aware of their freedom ---

Wherein is it said that One shall walk amongst them - which is prepared to bear witness of Me - and one which shall be qualified to set in order the affairs of the Nations -- I say: One shall come into thy midst which shall be as One prepared to set in order the affairs of State - and he shall bear witness of Me - for he shall KNOW the LAW - and be as one qualified to give unto the people counsel --

And they shall raise up and follow him knowingly and willingly - for he shall be as the One which is Sent that they be lifted up -- They shall hear his name for the first time in high places - as the One long expected - and they shall be sorely oppressed at the time of His pronouncements - for He shall be as One which hast come at the appointed hour -- When the hearts of men are sorely tried - heavy and sore - tearful shall be the women of all the lands - and fearful shall be the youths of all the lands - for they shall be confused and weary ---

While I say the old men shall shake their heads and deny Him in their fearfulness - and in their ignorance - they shall shout their slanderous sayings which they are so want to use against the fortune of men (their benefactors) -- Now it is come when they shall begin to bestir themself - for they have long awaited this day --

Yet they shall not see the finish of the Work this One shall do - for His reign shall be long - and good - and no man shall turn Him aside or overthrow Him - for He shall come in power and with great Strength - for He shall bear the Crown of Royalty -- He shall be as one on whose head rests the Crown of the House of Israel -- For He hast been as one prepared for long -- Long hast He awaited this day - when He might take up His reign -- So be it a triumphant reign - and mighty shall be His Work – I say: Behold ye the One which is to come - for He shall wear the Crown of Victory! --

For this does He come --

Recorded by Sister Thedra

I am the One

Sori Sori -- Be ye as one prepared to do that which I give unto thee to do - for it shall be for the good of ALL mankind -- And it shall be for their sake that I shall send One unto them which shall bear witness of Me - the Lord thy God -- Bear ye in mind that I AM THE ONE which hast held the Earth and the children thereof in the palm of Mine Hand and I am not of a mind to let Her go down into destruction!!

Therefore I shall do that which I WILL - and I am One on whose shoulders rests GREAT responsibility - for I shall choose the method by which I shall perform My Work - and I shall perform a Mighty Service unto ALL mankind ---

Therefore I shall do a strange thing - that they be healed of their blindness and deafness -- They shall <u>see</u> - and KNOW that they see ---

Therefore I say unto them: "Come and See - Come and Hear - Come and Know - and be healed" ---

Say unto them in Mine Name that "He is Come that ALL men be lifted up"-- And it is so -- Fortune thineself the Greater Part -- Bless thineself and I shall do Mine Part - for I Am the Way - the Truth and the Light --

Recorded by Sister Thedra

Deliverance

Sori Sori -- Hast it not been said that I the Lord God shall deliver up Mine people? and it is so -- So let it be -- And I say unto them: There shall be great times before the end of man's sojourn upon the Earth - for man hast not come into the fullness of his estate - he hast not as yet become that which he is fashioned to become - he hast not come into his own - for he shall yet become that for which he wast fashioned - when he first separated himself from his Source --

Yet he hast not separated himself - he hast but forgotten his Source - and in his forgetfulness he hast become one lost -- He hast wandered far - knowing not from whence he went out - from whence he come - neither whither he goest -- Now it is come when he shall walk knowingly - and he shall be glad for his knowing - he shall be as one returned unto his rightful estate -- So be it and Selah ---

Recorded by Sister Thedra

Behold the Glory of the Lord!

Sori Sori -- Hear ye this: I am He which is come into thy midst - which hast set up Mine banner - and which hast the power and authority to do that which I am come to do -- And for this shall the people of the Earth be lifted up - and the Name of Solen Aum Solen shall be exalted above ALL other -- For it is now come when men of Earth shall know they are not alone -- While there are many which stand by to assist - I say - they have waited for this day when men might be prepared to receive them ---

I say unto thee: Great and mighty is the Army of Light Workers - which have the power and the authority to bring about great and mighty changes upon the Earth -- And all men shall profit by that which shall be done - for it is for the good of all that they come at this time -- I say: Behold ye the Glory of the Lord thy God -- So be it that there shall be great and swift changes - and there shall be great clamoring amongst the nations - and the peoples --

Yet they shall burn their treaties - and they shall spill the blood of the innocent - in the determination to set free the people -- While I say unto them: Come ye forth and <u>BE</u> at Peace. I say: "COME YE FORTH AND BE AT PEACE"- - and they have not heeded Mine Voice -- Now they shall bestir themself - and they shall at last sit in council for the good of mankind - that the wounds of man be healed - and a new time - a new beginning shall be forth coming - for they shall see the folly of their way - and they shall sit as brothers one and all -- For this do WE come - that there be LIGHT - that they might KNOW PEACE -- Yet it shall be within THEM – and no man shall deny Me – neither shall any man make void MINE WORD – So be it and Selah ---

I Am He Which is Sent --

                          Recorded by Sister Thedra

One Shall Bear Witness

Sori Sori -- Hear ye the Voice of the Lord thy God - and bear ye witness of Him - for He seeks out all that will hear and heed -- So be it that I AM HE -- I Am He which is Sent that ALL men might be lifted up -- So be it that there shall come one within thy midst which shall bear witness of the Work which I do - for he shall know the Work and do it even as I do --

And no man shall set foot against him - for he shall be as iron against them - he shall bend not - neither shall he bow before their false gods -- He shall break bread with them - yet he shall need not eat thereof for he shall be sustained by that which they know not --So be it that they which know him shall know Me - for he shall be One with Me --

So be it and Selah --

Sori Sori -- Hear ye Me - and consider that which I say unto thee - for it is for the good of all that One shall be sent -- And he shall come before the "great and mighty" and they shall bear witness of him - and the power which he hast - which is given unto him by the Great and Mighty Council -- For he hast <u>proven</u> himself - and he shall bear witness of The Father Which hast Sent him -- Know ye that he comes to bear witness of <u>THE</u> FATHER - that men might be made strong in their knowing - that they might likewise bear witness of The Father Which hast ALL power ---

For that do I say unto thee: He shall come with <u>Authority</u> and Power. So be it he shall walk gently - quietly and humbly before men - and he shall send one before him to bear witness of him - and herald his coming -- Ye shall know him - for the MARK which he bears shall be written upon his brow -- He shall be as one of good account - and he shall not weary of well doing -- So be it he shall be fearless in his part. He shall bow unto no man - neither shall he compromise with the forces of evil -- He shall be his own Counselor and Advisor - for he shall know that which he is about -- And no man shall stop him - neither his Good Work --

So be it and Selah ---

Recorded by Sister Thedra

Behold the King of the Nations

Sori Sori -- Hear ye Me in this - and bear ye witness of Mine Word -- There shall be a great and mighty Call go out from the Inner Temple - and it shall be heard by many people - and they which hear shall respond knowingly - they shall make way for the Lord God Which shall bear upon His head the Crown of Victory -- I say unto thee: "Behold the King of the Nations"! - for He approaches from the East - and He beckons unto <u>All</u> men of <u>All</u> faiths - <u>All</u> creeds - <u>All</u> colors - And He shall abide with them as one of them - for He shall take up the garment of flesh - even as He laid down the garment of flesh -- He shall walk as man amongst men - and He shall wear the garments of men - for He shall appear in their midst as one of flesh even as they -- They shall know Him even as they know each other - as "man" -- While He shall put His hand to the plow - He shall bear witness of the Father Which hast Sent Him -- So be it and Selah --

Hail unto the King of Glory for He approaches even now -- Hail! Hail!! Unto the King of Glory!!

Blest art they which Know HIM!

Recorded by Sister Thedra

BLESS THINE BROTHER

Beloved: Ye shall be as one prepared to enter into the Holy of Holies - and ye shall abide with Me - for I shall give unto thee passport into Mine place of abode -- Now ye shall do that which I give unto thee to do in Mine name -- Ye shall wait upon Me - and ye shall walk with Me and be unafraid - for I shall be with thee all the way ---

Ye shall say unto them in Mine Name that – "I am come that all might follow where I go - and for this do say 'Come follow Me'" -- Now ye shall do the work which I give unto thee to do - and it shall be that which shall profit them which are want to follow Me -- Wherein is it said that - "I shall do a Mighty Work" - and for them which follow in the Way I lead them - they shall see and know that which I do --

And for them which are wont to serve self - they shall not see - neither shall they profit thereby - for they shall not know that which is being done. Is it not said that they put their hands before their eyes that they see not Wherein have they seen the Mighty Works which I have been doing? - Think they that I am asleep? ---

I say unto them: I am prepared for this day -- I am Come this day - that they be lifted up -- Let them be as ones prepared to go where I go. Let them be as ones prepared to follow Me - and they shall be glad!

So be it that I am He Which Knows them - even as I know Mine own Self - they deceive Me not - - I KNOW!

While they prattle as babes their foolish sayings as rigamaroles - I see them with all their furbish and weakness as little children at their games -- I say - they are weaklings and unknowing -- They are as the bigots and the ones which would be a light unto their feet -- They persecute and <u>would</u> <u>destroy</u> - yea - they would destroy -- Yet I say: I am with thee and I shall not deceive thee - neither shall I forsake Mine own -- I am with thee unto the end ---

While there are many which sleep still - I say: These shall awaken and come forth in due season ---

Yet they wait in vain - For that do I say - "Come forth" -- For they which do awaken <u>this</u> <u>day</u> - they shall be as the <u>host</u> - for they shall walk with Me knowingly -- Wherein is it said: I shall do Mine part and <u>then</u> take Mine leave -- Even as I come I shall go --

There are ones which shall never know of Mine coming - neither Mine going -- While they wait signs and wonders I shall come and go - leaving them in their darkness - for they shall be as the anti-christs - they shall be as the ones "left out crying at the gate" ---

For this do I say: Weary not thineself for the anti-christs - for they shall put their own foot forward and be their own porter -- So be it I say unto thee: Weary not thyself with their frivolities and with their wants and burdens -- Give unto thine brethren succor and cheer -- Yet ye carry him not on thine own back -- Bow before no man - and ask of no man his blessing - yet accept him as brother - and be glad for his blessing -- Add unto his blessings rejoice with him in his gladness - and give unto him as ye would receive of him --

So be it I shall join unto him that which has been unto him his fortune - and in this shall be profit -- Wherein is it given unto man to profit by his brother's inheritance? For this do I say: Rejoice with thine brother in his profit -- So be it that I shall add unto his in I thine name. On thine behalf shall I add unto his –

So be it and Selah ---

Anent the "Moon Shot"

Sori Sori -- Behold Mine Hand in this - for I Am the Lord thy God - and I am the One Sent that there be Light-- So let it be - I say - let it be!

I come that this day bring fruit - and I say unto thee: There is but One Lord God - and I AM HE -- So be it that I shall do a Work unknown to man -- While he is but the instrument of the Plan - he shall be as an efficient instrument -- And he shall come to know that he is not the Author of the Plan - that he stands not alone - that he is but an instrument in the Hand of the Infinite God - and by Whose Word he has been given <u>being</u> ---

While he (man) hast blundered - he shall now arise to heights unknown unto him -- He hast forgotten his heritage - and he shall come into his heritage within a short time ---

I say unto thee: Keep open thine eyes - hear ye that which I say unto thee - and be ye as one prepared - for I say - ye shall find that All is well within the Realm of Light -- Be ye as one with Me and I shall do as I have said I shall do - and ye shall come to see the wisdom of thy waiting --- So be it I KNOW that which I am about ---

Recorded by Sister Thedra

The Next Step?

Sori Sori -- Be ye as one prepared for that which is to come upon the Earth - for the time swiftly approaches when one shall go out from the Earth - without any fortune of the Earth - without any cumbersome material - without any gadgets -- He shall be free - "FREE" I say - free of all gadgetry -- He shall be as one prepared - he shall know the LAW and he shall come under the law - yet he shall be as one prepared to go out from the Earth as one free from the gravitation of the Earth - and free from the attraction of the Moon -- I say it shall be - and My Word shall not return unto Me void -- I have declared it so - So shall it be ---

Be ye as one prepared - for the time comes swiftly when man shall be liberated from the bonds of Earth - and he shall feel his spirit soaring as the bird - he shall be borne up as on gentle winds - he shall be as one free ---

I have spoken and I have been heard -- So be it and Selah --

I Am the Lord God - Sananda

Recorded by sister Thedra

Greater Horizons

Sori Sori -- Say unto them: The day arrives swiftly when one shall stand free from all gravitation of Earth - and he shall be as one free from the attraction of the Moon - he shall be as one free! I say as one free - for the law of gravity shall not bind Him unto the Earth -- He shall go and come freely - and stand as one free -- He shall be as one which has the crown of the Sun upon his head - he shall move freely thru the atmosphere - and he shall be as a trail blazer -- He shall be as the forerunner of that which is to be done - that which <u>shall</u> be done -- For this I say unto thee: Be ye as one prepared - for I say greater things than these shall ye do -- Wait no longer - be ye as ones prepared - for this is the day for which ye have waited - let thy waiting cease -- LOOK! SEE THE HAND OF GOD MOVE!! - for I say unto thee - It moveth swiftly and ye shall KNOW that which I say to be valid -- So be it and Selah.

Recorded by Sister Thedra

I am the Way

Sori Sori -- Let this day bring forth great fruit -- Let this day bring forth great Light -- Let this day bring forth great harvest -- Let this day bring forth great Knowledge -- Let this be the day of Light -- Let this day be the day of THE LORD -- For it is <u>now</u> come when the day of the Lord is here -- <u>This</u> is the day of The Lord -- I say: I shall walk amongst thee and I shall anoint them which seek the Light - for I am the Truth - The Light - The Way -- I say - I AM THE <u>WAY</u> ---

Follow ye Me - and I shall anoint thee and ye shall be AS one <u>anointed</u> - and ye shall know that ye have been touched -- So be it that Love fulfills all the Word - and I am come that the Word be fulfilled - for it <u>SHALL BE</u> - and it is by the GRACE of Mine Father Which hast sent Me -- So be it and Selah ---

Forget not that I AM come - that I AM with thee -- Look no longer for signs as of old -- Look up - see the Hand of "God" move -- I say It moveth upon the land - the seas - the air -- Wait not for another - for I come declaring: I AM HE - I AM COME - Look! See! and know ye that this is the Great Day promised thee so long ago -- I say: "THIS IS THE DAY OF THE LORD" - So be it as foretold of old ---

Let not thine preconceived ideas/ opinions - trip thee up - for it is written that 'man hast stumbled over his own toes' - he hast created his own bondage -- So be it I come that he might pick himself up and come forth as wast foreordained of The Father Solen Aum Solen ---

Recorded by Sister Thedra

I Shall Prove Myself

Sori Sori -- This is that for which they have waited -- This IS the day for which they have waited -- Now it is come when they shall be awakened - and they shall be as ones which have been awakened from a long and troubled sleep - for they have slept overtime ---

Now they shall arise and come forth as ones alert/ alive - and they shall know that THIS IS the day of THE LORD -- So be it they shall go about as ones awake and they shall be as ones alive -- They shall Know - and Know that they Know - so be it the Will of Mine Father which hast sent Me ---

Before the eyes of all men shall I prove Myself -- Before the eyes of ALL men shall I prove Myself - for I am come that they might awaken -- For this am I come - that they might Know - that they be free from bondage and dogma - that they might be free from all bondage -- So let it be -- Amen - and so it shall be ---

Fortune thyself the greater part - wait not for another -- I say: "Come YE - follow where I lead thee" Come - fear not - falter not -- Behold in Me that which I AM - for I shall not deceive thee -- Call unto the Father Solen Aum Solen Which hast given unto thee Life -- Ask that ye be given the Light - the Wisdom - the Truth -- Be ye alert - accept not the lesser - Ask of no man his blessing - ask of thy SOURCE and bless thyself -- For this have I said unto thee: "I AM HE which is sent that ye be blest as I have been blest" --

So be it -- So it is - and Selah --

Recorded by Sister Thedra

Greater the Revelation
Greater the Responsibility

Sori Sori -- Be ye as Mine Hand and My Foot made manifest - and go ye where I send thee -- Say ye that which I give unto thee to say - and ye shall be glad for that which shall be given unto thee ---

For hast it not been said that I - the Lord thy God - shall be unto thee all that ye have need of? So shall it be - let it be ---

I am come that it be so -- For this do I say - let it be as the Father hast willed it -- Wherein is it said that one shall come unto thee - and from out the Inner Temple cometh he -- He comes even as I - knowing from whence he cometh - and for which he cometh -- So be it and Selah.

I say unto thee: Man hast not seen that which is in store for him - for he hast not been as one prepared for such as now awaits him -- He hast as yet to prepare himself for the GREATER PART -- Yet it is now time that he arises - that he awakens and comes forth as the one prepared for <u>this</u> <u>day</u> - - This is the time spoken of <u>so</u> <u>long</u> ago - so long foretold - so long awaited -- This is the last days of the "Old Age" just past - the new age <u>so</u> - <u>so</u> <u>young</u> - <u>just</u> <u>beginning</u> -- And for this I say - there is an intervening time then the old and the new overlap - when the young and the old shall sup together - when the great and the small shall break bread together - when the Lion and the Lamb shall lie down together -- So shall it be in this day ---

Now in this day the Old shall throw off the shackles and put on the robe of freedom - and from the old shall come a NEW Freedom - a NEW Day - NEW AGE - and all the dross of the old shall be swept away - as the dross -- It shall be consumed by fire - and all which come thru the fire shall stand as the illumined - and they shall wear the Robe of the illumined -- They shall walk with sureness and with dignity -- They shall know from whence they come - and whither they goeth ---

I say unto thee: There are none which are so blind as the ones which see not -- There are ones which sit in high places - which wear the Crown of the Sun -- There are ones of lowly birth which wear the Robes of Royalty and walk with Me - these are Mine fellow workers -- They go where I go - they serve the Light and are not afraid -- So be it I say unto thee - I am with thee - I am with thee unto the end -- So be it and Selah ----

I am not afar off in some corner - I am not to be hidden -- I say I am not afar off -- Unto them which seek the Light - I shall reveal Mineself ---

Bear ye witness of Mine Words -

Bear ye Witness of Mine Words!

For I shall prove Mineself!

I am come that ye might bear witness of Me -- Now it is come when great things shall be revealed unto thee -- Yet with greater revelation comes greater responsibility -- Bear ye in mind - Greater the revelation, Greater the responsibility - so be it the law ---

Now ye shall do the work which I give unto thee to do - and ye shall have no fear - and ye shall let thy light so shine that they might see it from afar -- It is said: "They shall see it from afar" - so be it -- While it too is said - that a "prophet is without honor in his own house" it is the pity of it - for they are blinded by their own darkness - they see not - for they are as ones which put their own hands before their own eyes and say 'there is no light or I would see it'---

Now let them wait - for the time comes swiftly when they shall come crying for favors - they shall come begging for favors - and they shall say: Lord I have served Thee - day and night - I have supplicated Thee - I have donated my services unto Thee - why dost Thou not give unto me mine just due?

Mine own beloved: I say unto thee - such is blasphemy! I am not to be mocked! I am not asleep - I KNOW them - I know their hearts - I see them in their darkness asking favors of men - bidding for man's favors - seeking to deceive man - and themself -- They wear the cloak of the black magician - I say - I see them as ones naked! they deceive Me not! I say - I Know them for that which they are - they are blackguards - and vultures - they are as vipers - they are hypocrites and they serve their dragon's brew and offer it unto ME!! Yea - I say they think Me so foolish as to sip their brew? Nay - I enter not in!! They wait - they shall dine alone - for I enter not in -- They shall prepare a table fit for Me - then I shall come in and sup with them - and <u>then</u> they shall call Me <u>brother</u> then they shall invite Me in as such - and I shall enter in

Behold in Me the Light -- Behold ye that I AM - and I shall come in and give unto thee that which I have kept for thee -- For it is now come when ye shall throw off the old and take up the new - and it shall be becoming unto thee - for ye shall wear the Mantle of Gold - and its radiance shall be seen afar - and they shall behold it with eyes that see. They shall know that which they see - and rejoice for their sight -- I say behold ye the LIGHT WHICH I AM - FOR THAT I AM

The Father's Mercy & Grace

Sori Sori -- I am one which hast awaited this day -- Now that it is come I shall make known unto thee mineself - for it is given unto me to know thine longing and thy waiting -- I too know thine heart - I say: I know thine heart - and I know thy every thought -- While it is given unto thee to be of strong heart and mind - I say thine physical body is weak - and it shall endure much pain ere the end -- Yet let it go on record as being fortuned unto thee to be the pioneer which hast blazed the trail for the One which is called the Wayshower - Sananda - Son of God -- I say thou hast pioneered - for first wast thou given the name Sananda so many years ago --

Now ye shall see and know what hast been accomplished by thy service unto the Light - the race of man -- The fortune of them which receive Him shall be great and glorious - for I say unto thee ALL which receive Him and of Him shall receive that which He hast for them -- May they which cry Lord Lord - be acceptable unto Him - for it is said: Not all which cry Lord Lord shall be heard - for they have not prepared themself for to receive of Him -- Now I speak unto thee of the next part, the part which shall be next - the part of Grace -- Grace is that which is given unto thee thru and by the Mercy of Our Father Solen Aum Solen.

Wherein hast man been given Grace? Wherein hast he found Mercy? I say - it is a bestowal of the Father - and by His Grace shall ye be brot into the place wherein I abide - for it is by His Grace that I am come unto thee/ by His Grace that ye receive me - and by His Grace that I am prepared to enter into thine place of abode -- While I am free to go and come - it is by His Grace that I AM free - that ye shall be freed -- Now ye shall come to know the meaning of "Freedom" -- Wherein hast man of Earth been free? I say he is bound! and he knows not the pity of his bondage --

While I know the pity of it I know the joy of freedom - the joy is beyond man's imagination - for nothing he can image can compare with the joy of the one which hast earned his freedom -- Now I say - rejoice with them which earned their freedom - the ones which now reach out a helping hand unto thee -- Praise ye the name of Solen Aum Solen - let thy song ring out thru the Cosmos - let it resound thruout the Earth, let it fill the / - let it fill the hills - the valleys - and blest shall they be which hear thy song - for it shall be heard - IT SHALL BE! There shall be great joy when it is heard -- I say let them which have ears to hear - hear - let them pick up the Glad Song and rejoice with all that have heard - for there shall be a Glad day when all shall sing together - as when the Sons of God sang together -- IT SHALL BE! IT SHALL BE!!

Praise Ye the Name of Solen Aum Solen -

(The Good Brother)

The Door Keeper of the Temple of Light

Sori Sori -- Mine hand I place upon thine head and I bless thee with Mine presence -- I bring with Me One which hast been prepared within the Inner Temple -- He hast been given the part which is now revealed unto thee -- He hast prepared himself for the blessings bestowed upon him this day -- Forget not - as a man prepares himself so he becomes - let it be for it is the law ---

Wait upon Me the Lord thy God and I shall bless thee as I have blest him -- So be it he serves with his whole being - he gives of himself that others might be blest as he hast been blest -- So be it and Selah -- I say he hast blest himself by his obedience and selfless service -- So be it and Selah ---

Fortune thyself the love and service of this one which I bring -- So be it that he hast within his hand the power to bless thee - for this do I bring him -- Ye shall know him as the "Good Brother"

Beloved: I come unto thee this day as a Brother prepared to bring thee into the place of mine abode - and I say unto thee: I am he which cometh in love and peace -- I come as one prepared -- For this day let it be said - I am he which cometh in peace even as mine beloved Brother Sananda -- While it is given unto me to stand before Him with humble heart and bowed head - I say I am swift to obey His every command - and command He shall - and obey I shall --

I shall give unto thee a part which shall be different from the other parts - yet it shall be placed with all other parts - and they which have gone thru the other parts shall receive this one - and unto them I say: Be ye as one prepared for the Greater part - for I shall be as one prepared to come unto thee - and I shall give unto thee that which is so necessary for the entrance into the place wherein I abide -- I tell thee for a certainty that I am the one which shall bring thee into the place wherein I abide -- And before thou canst enter into the Holy of Holies thou shall come unto this place wherein I am "Door Keeper"-- I say ye shall NOT enter into the Holy of Holies without first passing thru mine place of abode - it is the law ---

For this do I say unto thee mine beloved: I come unto thee that they too might know the Law -- I say - abide ye by the law - for none enter any other way - there is NO OTHER WAY -- Hear ye me and be ye as one prepared - for this have I come -- Bless thyself by thy preparation.-

While I say there is no other way - I say: Choose ye which way ye go -- Yet it be mine part to say - any other way leads unto darkness and destruction - "damnation" if you will -- Therefore I say: Seek ye first the Light - Truth - and all things shall be revealed - IT SHALL BE - for this do I come even as my beloved Brother Sananda ---

Now it is with Great concern that I speak of the ones which falter upon the path at this point -- I say at this point many fail - for they fear, they faint - and turn aside -- Pity is the plight of the one which turns aside - I say - pity is his plight! The path is not smooth - the way is steep and rugged - yet the Light shineth within the Temple wherein I abide -- I say unto thee: Sorrow and pain cometh not into of the place wherein I am - <u>wherein I am</u>!

I am one which has overcome - I have found the way into the place wherein there is no sorrow - no darkness - wherein all things are known wherein we praise Solen Aum Solen with our Being -- I tell thee of many things - yet words cannot tell thee of the joy of one which enters into the Temple of Light ---

Man of Earth knows no such joy - yet when he renounces all to follow HE - which IS COME - shall be filled with joy - for He hast prepared the Way - He hast brot me here -- Now I turn unto thee to give mine hand unto thee that ye might Know as I Know - <u>for</u> <u>this</u> <u>am</u> <u>I</u> <u>come.</u> So let it be as the Father hast willed it ---

I speak that all might know - yet to the few I give mine hand - for the many reject me --The few which are prepared shall receive me and accept mine assistance -- While I say I am the One Sent at this point - this time - I say others shall ye find which shall bring unto thee greater and Greater Light - even tho ye shall not receive of them before thou hast <u>passed</u> <u>thru</u> <u>this</u> <u>door</u> ---

So be it I extend mine hand in loving service to all mankind - I am at the service of ALL -- Yet unto them which accept the service - the love - I am he which shall bring them safely into this place - the Temple of Light -- So be it and Selah --

Recorded by Sister Thedra

Mine "Plowmen"

Sori Sori -- By Mine hand shall ye be led - and by Mine own hand shall I lead thee every step of the way --

Now ye shall put thine pen to paper and record that which I say unto thee -- Let them know that which I say unto thee - let them know that which I say - for I am now speaking out that all men might come to know that they are not alone ---

Think they that I have been as one in bondage - in darkness?

I say I AM the LIVING GOD -

I AM HE which hast caused the worlds to be formed -

I AM HE which hast set them into motion -

I AM HE which hast peopled them -

I AM HE which hast formed the worlds yet unknown unto thee -

I AM HE which hast brot forth great changes - and great civilizations I have caused to be brot forth as the manifestation of Mine own works -- Then as ever before thee - there hast come and gone greater civilizations than the one thou now knowest - for there are changes ever taking place - sifting and sorting - making and unmaking. As to perfection - none hast reached perfection as yet ---

While it is said: "THE KINGDOM OF GOD SHALL BE ESTABLISHED UPON THE EARTH" - it is not accomplished -- And for this have I called forth many a Nobleman - many a great and generous man - unknown for his greatness amongst the men of the world -- I have set them apart from all others - giving them that part for which they have prepared themself - - These I have declared the forerunners of a greater civilization - a greater part shall they have in the "New Day" for their preparation ---

I say - the "Pioneers" I have sent forth to blaze the trail for them which shall follow -- They which follow shall reap that which hast been sown by the pioneers -- Their rewards shall be no less - for their part shall be the harvest - and it shall be great indeed!

Now that I have called forth a mighty host to partake of the harvest.- I say unto Mine "Plowmen": Come forth - that ye might receive thy reward -- And stand ye forth and see the work of thy hand - and know ye that I have brot thee forth that the law be fulfilled - that each might bring forth the fruit of his labor and receive his share - the reward of his labor ---

Blest be the labor of his hand - for I have set the laborer over the Kings of the Earth -- I have exalted Mine Servants over the crowned heads of all the lands -- I have prepared a table before them in the presence of the ones which persecute them -- I have prepared a place for them wherein they shall know peace -- I say: BLEST ARE MINE SERVANTS - for they shall abide with Me - and they shall know peace.

Prepare thineself for the day of rejoicing cometh swiftly -- I say: Arise and come with Me and I shall glorify thee - as with the ROYAL RAIMENT I shall gird thee about - and swiftly shall ye be as one which hast found thy way into the place which is prepared for the servants of the LORD GOD - Host of Hosts ---

Lord of Lords I Am -- Come as on the air - borne as on the wings of Light - for I AM THE LIGHT - I AM the WING which shall bear thee away ---

I speak as one which knows - for I AM the Knower - the doer - for there is none other which knows that which I KNOW - AS I KNOW -

for I stand as one on higher ground - above thee I stand as on the mountain top -- I stand - while thou hast thine feet in the shadow within the valley ---

Now I say: ARISE! COME UP! COME UNTO ME! - Stand with Me as one with Me - and I shall shew thee that which thou hast not seen. I say: BEHOLD THE GLORY OF THE LORD THY GOD! ---

Bear ye witness of Me -- Bear ye witness of Mine sayings - and know ye that I am with thee ---

I shall not forsake thee - neither shall I forget that which I have said unto thee ---

Be ye at Peace and Poise -- For this have I spoken unto thee ---

Recorded by Sister Thedra

Lay Down Thine Arms

Sori Sori -- Be ye as the hand of Me and make ye known unto the people that which I say unto thee - and fear not that I leave thee unto them - for I say - ye shall not be alone in this - for I shall direct thee and protect thee -- So be it I AM the Director - I Am He which is Sent - and there shall be no mistake in this -- Fortune thyself that which I give unto thee to do - and I shall uphold thee ---

For this day let it be said that I the Lord God speaketh - and I speak out that all men might come to know that which I say ---

Let it be as the law requires - for it is lawful that they hear - that they know - that they act according unto the law -- They shall put aside their weapons - and their fears shall be as nought -- They shall walk as brothers - knowing themself to be brothers - KNOWING THEMSELF TO BE BROTHERS - AS ONE FLESH - ONE SPIRIT! ---

For this do I say: LAY DOWN THINE ARMS - AND COME - FOLLOW ME! - and I shall give unto thee PEACE which shall abide within thy heart! HEAR YE ME - O - MAN OF EARTH! HEAR YE ME - ALL YE CHILDREN OF EARTH - for I AM NOT TO BE DENIED! I say: YE SHALL HEAR and YE SHALL

HEED MINE WORD - <u>lest ye perish</u>! While I say: "Lest ye perish" - I say: it is thy own undoing --

I COME THAT YE PERISH NOT!!

Fear not that I betray thee -- Yet unto them which heed not Mine Word I say: "YE BETRAY THINE OWN SELF"---

For this do I say: Come ye forth and speak ye the word which shall make of ALL MEN BROTHERS -- Give not the bitter cup unto thy brother -- Lift him up and be ye not fearful of him - for where there is LOVE there is no fear -- Be ye one with Me and ye shall have no fear for I AM THY SHIELD AND THY BUCKLER - THY PROTECTOR.

For this do I say: COME - SEEK YE FIRST THE KINGDOM - and I shall bring thee into the place wherein I abide -- I come from out the place wherein there is perfect peace - and wherein ye shall not enter until thou hast prepared thineself for entrance ---

I say: BEHOLD YE THE LIGHT OF THE WORLD!

Behold ye the darkness of man within the world of man! -- See ye the way of man - -

SEE YE THE LIGHT WHICH I AM ---

I say: See ye the difference - and choose ye the way ye should go - I say COME - and ye stand as one with feet of lead -- Bear thine arm - and raise thine voice -- Let it be known where ye stand -- Fearlessly ye shall speak - and ye shall not speak falsely - for I know where ye stand.- I KNOW ---

Be ye as one which hast Mine hand upon thee - and I shall bless thee - and do that which I have said I will do -- So be it and Selah ---

Recorded by Sister Thedra

To Whom?

Beloved: Upon Mine Holy Mt. I stand - and see them as ones chained bound by their own legirons - with their forms and customs which hast bound them -- They are filled with fear - fear of opinions - opposition oppression one with the other/ against the other -- They <u>bargain</u> for a puny penny - they ask of their brother their sweat - their labor for bread They ask of their Benefactors their all -- They barter, bargain in human sacrifice - FOR WHAT?

What are they? What have they accomplished in their journey within the Earth? Have they become free? Have they freed themself from their bondage? To whom do they turn for surcease? To whom do they pray for relief? To whom do they account for their deeds? To whom do they give allegiance? To whom do they turn in the time of affliction? To whom do they return in the end? To whom do they give penance? To whom the credit - to whom the sacrifice?

Let them ask themself these questions - truthfully - and they shall be as ones prepared for the next part -- Ponder upon these things and be ye as ones alert - for I say unto them: they have bound themself - and they say unto themself - "I am FREE" -- They make of themself liars - for they know not FREEDOM!

I say they are in bondage! I am come to deliver them out - yet I say they shall will it so -- So be it as they will it -- Yet I say - that they shall know the law - and abide thereby - for I am the law - I AM THE LAW AND I AM NOT BOUND BY IT - for nothing binds ME - I AM FREE I KNOW WHAT FREEDOM IS! And when thou hast become <u>free</u> - no man can make of thee slave or servant!

I say: 'Ye shall live the law" - and too I say: "That which ye bind shall bind thee - for it is the law" -- Ye bind thyself by binding other. By freeing others - ALL OTHERS - ye unbind thyself ---

LOVE THEM FREE - give unto none the bitter cup - give unto none a tack for his shoe - give unto none a sorry word - and give unto all as they should give unto thee/ as ye would have them give unto thee.

I say ye shall do unto him as ye would have him do unto thee - ask nothing of him that ye would not give unto him -- Be ye as one circumspect in all thy dealings - all thy ways ---

Watch each word which proceeds from thy mouth - and weigh it carefully - for as the <u>'virus'</u> - as the 'bacteria' it goes out - and takes form - and it lives - lives upon that which is called "THOUGHT"

Within the eth doth it find lodging - and multiply - it has power - and it is a living thing - and it finds root within the human mind -- As the seed dropt from the beak of a bird finds lodging within the earth soil - and is nourished and grows - so does the unsuspected word which goeth out from thy lips - and ye are unaware of this power--

I say - ye shall become aware of the power of the spoken word - and ye shall use it to bless thyself - for it is the law that they return unto thee - bearing fruit of like measure - yet increased a thousand times! Be ye as ones forewarned and fore armed - for I say now - as the boomerang they shall return unto thee this day ---

Be ye silent - and give unto thyself rest from speech - for it is energy. Use it to glorify the Father in the Earth -- Give unto Him all praise and the glory - and call unto Him with all thy heart - mind - and soul for <u>wisdom</u> - and ye shall not be denied or oppressed- I say - He shall deliver thee out -- So be it that I am come that ye may be delivered and I bring a Host with Me ---

I AM - Sananda - The Nazarine - The Wayshower ---

Recorded by Sister Thedra

The Shepherd & The Flock Shall Be as One

Sori Sori -- Be ye as the hand of Me made manifest - and say unto them in Mine name - that there shall be GREAT changes -- Changes shall be made in the name of Him which is come - and which shall reign supreme -- For it is now come when the hand which is to the plow shall see the harvest ripen - and reapt -- For the day cometh swiftly when the

Shepherd shall be as one of the flock - and He shall stand with the flock and the "Flock" shall know Him as one of "them"-- Yet it is said: "I now walk amongst them - I anoint their head with oil - I bless them and call them by name"- and none shall deny them the fortune which I have kept for them -- So be it it is a fortune not of the world - yet it is greater than all earthly fortunes -- Placed in Mine hand is the authority and power to do that which is to be done -- And I say: BLEST IS HE which puts his hand to the plow -- Blest is he which goes into the field for to sow - for I shall give unto him sustenance -- He shall overcome -- Blest is he which endures - for he shall overcome ---

Blest is the one which overcomes - for he shall see God - I say "HE" shall see God ---

Let this be Mine Word unto them which have ears to hear - for unto them I shall speak/ I shall tell them that which shall profit them - and they shall learn the secrets of the elements - the "Secrets" which hast not yet been revealed - - And then - they shall break the bonds of darkness/ ignorance - and they shall go where I go - and then they shall know as I know - and then they shall have no fear - for they shall be wise indeed! They which will to follow Me shall walk as one unafraid, fearing neither man/ beast/ wind/ rain/ the storm of the land or the seas for no harm shall come nigh unto him ---

I say: Mine hand shall sustain him at all times - and I shall make of him a spirit above all flesh - and he shall not be bound by flesh - for flesh shall have no power over him -- He shall walk and fear not -- He shall walk the galaxies as one free -- He shall be as the "FREE" and he shall know his SOURCE OF BEING - and he shall rejoice forevermore.

Now I say unto thee: Come - follow ye Me and I shall show GREATER things than thou hast dreamed of - for all thy longings shall be no more -- All thy seeking shall be filled - for ye shall stand as one illumined -- So be it and Selah ---

Behold ye the hand of God - See it move - and be glad - for I AM COME that ye be lifted up -- So be it that I have spoken - and ye have heard Me ---

Recorded by Sister Thedra

They Shall Know the True from the False

Sori Sori -- Be ye as the hand of Me and say unto them as I would say: "I am come this day that there be light - that they might come to know the true from the false" - for false there be - false there hast been - and false there shall be -- Yet the "false" shall be brot to light and exposed for that which it is -- And no longer shall the "false" be under cover - for it shall be uncovered!

I say - the "false" shall be exposed - and they shall know the TRUE from the false!!

I bring unto them TRUTH - for I AM the TRUTH and the LIGHT. From out the Light I come! I bear witness of Mine Father which hast sent Me ---

I come that I might find Mine own/ and Mine own shall know Mine voice and come unto Me - and they shall do Mine bidding and rejoice in the doing - for they shall know that I am He which sustains them --

I say unto Mine own: COME! COME YE FORTH! Come and be counted - for I shall claim Mine own - and no man shall say Me NAY!

I say: Mine own shall come forth and rejoice that this day is come and they shall be glad -- Hear ye Mine children - let thine heart rejoice - for I am come this day that ye be free from ALL bondage - all darkness -- I say Come - Come follow Me - and I shall shew thee that which ye have not seen.

I shall give unto thee as ye have not received - for I have kept the greater part for thee for this day-- It is said: "As ye are prepared - so shall ye receive" -- So be it and Selah ---

I bless thee with Mine presence - and I give unto thee of Mineself that ye be sustained - and that ye be brot out of bondage -- And I say: "No greater love hast any man than this - no greater part hast any man than to bring forth that which hast gone out from Mine place of abode". For this am I come - for this am I speaking out this day - for THIS IS THE DAY of deliverance for them which seek the Light which I AM. Be ye as one on whose head I place Mine hand - and I say unto thee: Be ye as one prepared to go where I go - for I am one with Mine Father and to Him I shall return -- So be it it and Selah ---

Recorded by Sister Thedra

No Man Knows the Greater Reward

Sori Sori -- For this day - let it be known that the time is come when great shall be the work which shall be done thru and by Mine servants. Great shall be the labor of their hands - yea greater than all other - for have I not said: "'Greater things than these shall ye do?" Is it not so? I say: IT IS SO! So let it be - for I have declared unto them that I am come that it be so -- I am not to be denied - I am not to be staid - for I am come that they be prepared for the Greater part -- The Greater part shall be their reward - the reward which no man knoweth which hast not as yet received it -- Now I say unto thee: I have received Mine reward - therefore I shall speak of the "Greater Part" as One which KNOWS -- For this do I speak - that ye be as one prepared to go where I go - for I go unto Mine Father which hast sent Me ---

Hold high Mine banner - walk ye after Me - and ye shall be lead into the place wherein I am -- Not all thy learning is sufficient to thy salvation - for I say: It shall profit no man - that which he learns within the great and wondrous institutions of Earth - and knows not <u>THE WAY</u> of "THE ONE SENT" ---

For it behooves him to put aside his <u>ideas</u> and opinions of Me and about Me - and HEAR that which I have to say unto him THIS DAY.

Yet there are ones which claim to know Me - yet they close Me out this day -- Wherein have they become wise? Wherein have they become useful unto Me? I say unto them: "Come follow Me - and ye shall be obedient unto the call - ye shall hear Mine Voice and respond unto it"-- Let no man turn thee aside - and be ye as one responsible for thine own calling - thine own work which shall be allotted unto thee -- <u>Fortune</u> <u>thineself</u> <u>the</u> <u>Greater</u> <u>part</u> -- So be it I await the day when I might touch ALL mankind - and that they know they have been touched. Then they shall be glad - for this do I say: "Hear ye Me and respond unto Mine Words" ---

Fortune thyself the Great reward which is the fortune of the fold of the "One Sent"- and ye shall hold high the banner which I bring/ ye shall fail not!

Ye shall walk with surety - for I shall go all the way with thee - and ye shall do that which I do - ye shall go where I do - and ye shall be glad - for I say unto thee - ye knowest not the Greater reward which awaits thee---

Praise ye tha Name of Solen Aum Solen ---

Recorded by Sister Thedra

I Come Declaring

Sori Sori -- Hear ye the Words of the LORD thy GOD - for I declare unto thee <u>this</u> day: "I am HE which hast been thy Benefactor - thy Shield and thy Buckler ---

Bring unto Me thyself in wholely surrender - that ye might do the things which I do - that ye might go where I go -- So be it that I am One which hast given of Myself that ye be brot out of bondage ---

I come declaring unto thee: thou art the SON OF THE MOST HIGH LIVING GOD - and I stand before thee as the "ONE SENT" - So be it that I AM HE ---

I speak that ye might hear -- So let it be known that which I say -- So be it it shall profit them to hear that which I say - for My Voice shall be raised in this day -- And unto all which obey Mine call I shall give unto them greater gifts - and they shall be glad! So be it that I shall raise My VOICE against the ones which put words into My mouth - for I shall spew them out and I shall be unto them as a mighty fire - I shall burn with GREAT FURY that which I shall spew out - for I say; they which put words into MY MOUTH do blaspheme against the HOLY SPIRIT ---

I say: "THEY BLASPHEME AGAINST THE HOLY SPIRIT!!

So be it I am not of the darkness - I know from whence I come - whither I goeth - and I ask man no favors -- I put Mine hand upon thy head - and I pronounce the WORD which shall be unto thee great strength - power and authority - for I come in the name of Mine Father Which hast SENT ME ---

I say: "they" shall sit within judgement - and put their foot against thee - yet I say - I shall lift thee up and I shall do a mighty work thru thee - for I shall give unto thee power and authority which I shall entrust unto thee - for thine loyalty and preparedness hast been proven - and I shall remember thee in the days of thy rendering service unto thy fellow man - for inasmuch as ye do it unto them - ye do it unto Me -- So be it and Selah --

Hold high thine head and bow down unto no man - for I am the One which shall bless thee and sustain thee -- Be ye as one forever blest ---

Recorded by Sister Thedra

Concerning Man's Freedom

For this day let it be said that Solen Aum Solen is the Father Which has sent ME -- I come declaring unto thee the Truth and Light -- The Light of the world Am I - I AM HE which lighteth the way -- Wherein is it said that - "I Am come that they have Light"-- So be it - I speak as of old - and unto all which have ears to hear I speak -- I say unto them that they shall hear the WORD - and they shall have the Word given in this day - and in this time which is now -- And ye shall bear witness of the Word given THIS DAY - for this is the day long foretold - when man shall be as ones lifted up - when man shall break the bounds of Earth and soar into realms unknown - when man shall be free from the gravity of the Earth and free from the attraction of the moon ---

I say - the attraction of the moon shall no longer bind man - for he shall be as one free from the attraction thereof -- So be it I shall bring unto man a new Song - for he shall be as one prepared to hear the NEW TUNE -- I say - as he is prepared - so shall he receive -- So be it and Selah ---

Forget not that I am He which comes in the name of Mine Father Solen Aum Solen ---

While many call out the names given of old - I say - they shall come to know the Name of the Father Which IS SOLEN AUM SOLEN -- The Name given unto the Children of their fore-fathers was that which was theirs for that day -- Now I say - their forefathers hast rejected the Father for the most part - and they have rejected Me and denied Me as of old -- While I come bearing witness of the SAME FATHER - and offering unto them their salvation as of old - they deny Me as of old - and they spit on the Word - while I stand before them offering unto them the CUP -- I say - I hold within Mine hand the Crystal Goblet - they have but to reach out and accept it in the Name of the Father Which hast sent Me ---

I give unto thee the Name of Solen Aum Solen for this day - that ye might have GREATER understanding than "the forefathers" of old ---

I come that ye be as ones prepared for the <u>Greater</u> part ---

Now I stand - hands out stretched - calling unto thee: Come! Come! for I have the Cup prepared - I have the place prepared - and I am prepared to receive thee unto Mine place of abode ---

Unto ALL I say: COME - yet I say - few there be which heed Mine call - and walk in the way I walk ---

Come - Come - follow Me and ye shall be glad - for I shall show thee many new things - and ye shall delight in the way of the Lord thy God -- So be it and Selah -- I am He which knows the delights of Heaven - the delights of Paradise - for I am not of the Earth - I am come from out the realm of Light that ye be delivered out -- Fortune thineself Mine Way - and count thyself amongst the redeemed - the illumined - and no more shall ye wander in bondage ---

Blest are they which go where I go ---

Blest are they which come into the place which is prepared for them.

For this do I say COME! -- Let it be as The Father hast willed it --

Recorded by Sister Thedra

The Law

Sori Sori -- <u>This</u> day I say unto thee: Bless thineself - fortune unto thyself the Greater part - and be ye as one forever blest -- Give unto "them" this Mine Word - for this is that which I give unto thee for them.

It is now come when they shall bless themself by that which they do -- They shall go about The Father's business even as I - and they shall give unto no man the <u>bitter</u> cup -- They shall sit at their council tables as brothers - and they shall forget their wars - and they shall put forth their hand in fellowship - and be as brothers ALL ---

They shall be as ones which have given themself unto the plan -- They shall earn the right to call themself masters - for they shall first learn well the law and abide within and by it -- They shall do that which I do - and I say unto thee - We of the Mighty Council abide by the law! We are fortuned the Greater part - yet We are not above the GREATER LAW -- In each realm there exists a law governing that realm - and for this I say unto them: "Heed ye the <u>law</u> - the LAW under which man of Earth comes" -- This law sets forth that all are of one Source - one life and therefore no man has the right to take from another his right to exist in flesh/ his vehicle -- While it is not given unto man to destroy life - he can and does destroy the vehicles which comes about thru and by this law of which I speak ---

Now I speak unto thee of the law of life which exists upon the orb of Earth ---

All are <u>one</u> and therefore come under the law of "THE ONE"---

Gracious is "THE ONE" -- Merciful is this law - and none transgresses it without adjustment - without price - I say - there is a price!

Each shall learn the price - and pay unto the last farthing - no man escapes! None - I say!

For this I say: "<u>Bless thyself by obedience unto the law which hast sustained thee</u> - for it is just - JUST I SAY!! ---

While they cry for mercy - I say - they forget in their crying that they are not blameless -- They have set into motion that which <u>now</u> prompts their cries-- Let them learn that which they must - for a lesson learned is a lesson earned - it is the law ---

For this hast the law been given - and for this hast it been said many times:

<u>Obedience</u> unto the law is the first requirement of the Candidate for initiation into the "Secrets of the Most High" -- For from Obedience comes <u>trustworthiness</u> - from trustworthiness comes greater responsibility - from greater responsibility comes greater things - greater illumination - greater parts - higher heights to be attained -- Let it be - for it is so -- When a man hast proven himself trustworth - he is given greater responsibility - and with that - greater trust/ greater illumination -- So be it that I watch with great joy the ones who walk with their head high - their backs strait - their hands to the plow - their compass set and which know wherein they are staid ---

I bless <u>them</u> - for these are Mine servants which do the will of Mine Father -- So be it and Selah ---

For this I say: Walk with thy head high and follow ME - for I AM the Light which lighteth man's way --

Recorded by Sister Thedra

The Productive Branch

Sori Sori -- For this day let it be said that he which puts his hand unto the plow and turns back - shall be as one which betrays himself - for he shall be as the pruned branch which bears no fruit -- He shall be plucked up and cast into the fire - as the branch which brings forth no fruit ---

For this do I say unto them which come out from among the ones which have no knowledge of Me: Bring thyself as one prepared to do that which I give unto thee to do -- Hear that which I say - and be ye as one prepared to do that which I give unto thee to do ---

Be ye humble of heart - be ye steadfast - be ye of ONE MIND - and forget not that I am thy Shield and thy Buckler -- So be it and Selah -- For this do I say COME - for this do I say: "Be ye as one prepared"- for I know where I go - I know thee - I know thy preparation - and it is sufficient that ye obey the LAW which I give unto thee -- For this do I speak of obedience -- While it is not given unto thee to know the fullness of the law - ye do know that which I ask of thee -- So be it that I require nothing more of thee than obedience unto the law which I reveal unto thee -- I am the Lord thy God - and I Am Sent of Mine Father that ye be prepared -- So let it be ---

Recorded by Sister Thedra

The Need of the Times

Sori Sori -- This is Mine Word for <u>this</u> day: Mine Word is sacred - and given for a divine purpose - and I speak with purpose -- I know the purpose - and I am aware of the times - and the need of the times ---

Now I say: There is great need for Me to speak out -- I speak that <u>all</u> might come to know that I speak - for in the times past they were deaf unto the Word - Few there was which <u>listened</u> - and I say unto thee today there are <u>few</u> which listen ---

Yet I too say - that their ears shall be opened - their eyes shall be opened - and they shall be touched and know that they have been touched ---

They shall no longer bow before the ones which have NOT been touched - and ask for their blessings - for they have been sorely oppressed by the ones which call themself the "Select" and the <u>righteous</u> ---

I say - the foolish shall no longer hold a people in bondage by their foolishness of preaching -- They shall first know that which is <u>right</u> - then they shall practice right-eousness - and they shall walk in the way of the Lord knowingly - dealing justly with ALL MEN -- And they shall be as ones humble before ALL MEN - and they shall be as ones blest ---

For this do I say: Follow ye ME - for I am the Way Shower - I am come that they might find their way - and no man cometh unto the Father save thru ME ---

For I am the One Sent into flesh -- <u>Flesh</u> <u>of</u> <u>Earth</u> have I taken upon the / eternal I AM -- The garment of flesh have I taken - that man of Earth might come to know that I AM -- So be it I am not alone - for I have brot with Me others which have taken the garments of flesh that they might walk with man and be seen and counted -- While I say: The Unseen Host count ever greater in number than all the Earthlings of all the ages!

I say the Mighty Host which come with Me number greater than that of Earth -- While ye see <u>them</u> not - they are not unaware of thy going and coming - they watch and guide with LOVE and WISDOM. They impose not on thy free will - They are aware of thy will at ALL TIMES ---

So be it that they give assistance when and where needed - for the good of ALL MANKIND ---

They - when necessary - come as the individual - Mentor/ guide or assistant -- Yet they answer not the selfish call - the selfish prayer - for they come even as I – that ALL men be lifted up ---

Hast it not been said that I come that there be Light?

So let it be for the GOOD of ALL -- I am HE which comes to deliver men from darkness/ bondage -- For this do I say: Be ye alert unto Mine Voice - be ye alert and follow where I lead thee - so shall I guide thee aright -

Be ye blest to follow where I go - for I go unto Mine Father which hast Sent ME ---

So be it and Selah

Why? O, Man

Beloved of my being: I speak into thee as one of the Great and Mighty Council -- I speak unto thee from out the realms of Light - wherein there is <u>no</u> mystery - yet it is given unto thee to be in the place wherein there <u>is</u> mystery - for all things are not as yet revealed unto thee ---

It is given unto man to walk in darkness - without revelation -- Now it is come when greater revelation shall be given unto thee ---

It is for this that WE of the Mighty Council hast revealed Ourself unto thee ---

Now ye shall be as one which hast the power and the authority to speak for US - for We shall give unto thee a part for <u>them</u> which are of a mind to receive it - and they shall accept that which is prepared for them -- And as they are prepared - so shall they receive - it is the LAW.

Wherein is it said that they which <u>receive</u>* the Word shall be blest. I say they shall be blest! And it is so ---

While it is given unto and for all - I see them rejecting it and turning from the WORD which is given unto them for <u>their</u> <u>own</u> <u>sake</u> -- And for that matter - We see them suffer and cry for help - knowing not that it is proffered unto them - yet they accept not that which WE have given in Mercy and in WISDOM

For their sake do We say: Blest are they which accept Our assistance -- We know their needs - their frailties - their strength - and We see their despair - and yet they cry out unto their unknown gods for assistance ---

WHY - O - MAN! hast thine suffering been so long?

For this hast many been sent - that it might be ended -- Now it is come when ye might be freed from all thine miseries-- Wherein is it said: "This is THE DAY OF DELIVERANCE"-- Ye have not begun thine way within the place wherein ALL things are known - ye are as yet in the land of forgetfulness - ye know not as WE know - yet ye <u>think</u> thyself sufficient -- It is <u>not</u> SO! For without revelation thou art in darkness and despair!

DESPAIR I SAY!! - without revelation thou art in darkness -- WE of this Mighty Council have opened wide the DOORS of REVELATION that ye be enlightened -- Accept the Light which We bring-- Be ye as one acceptable unto US and be as one prepared for to receive of US - and to administer unto them which know not -- For this is it said: "Many are called and few are chosen"- for few there be are prepared to receive of US --

There are <u>many</u> which reject THE WORD and turn a deaf ear unto US while they are attentive unto the clamor and glamor of the <u>lesser</u> - the voice of the "dead" - the unknowing ones -- Unto these We say: Listen not unto the liars and the ones which would <u>hold</u> them in bondage - for they are not of THE LIGHT - they too are bound in darkness -- They are not freed from bondage - they are of the dark - knowing not -- For this do we say: "Seek the Light"- first seek the Light and it shall not be hidden from thee -- Be ye blest to receive of US -- For this are We now speaking ---

While it is given unto thee to seek wisdom - it is given unto US to lead thee safely into <u>greater</u> <u>planes</u> - greater heights -- Greater Light and Greater Knowledge shall be given as thine strength increases -- So be it and Selah ---

*Receiving means accepting/ believing/ applying-

Recorded by Sister Thedra

The Word is Not to Be Set Aside

Sori Sori -- For this day let it be understood that I the Lord God give unto thee this Word - and it shall not be made void - for it is the WORD OF GOD - and the WORD <u>IS</u> <u>THE</u> <u>WORD</u> - not to be set aside or made void -- Let it be understood that the time is now come when many cry for peace - for light - yet they seek surcease from their suffering and peace - within the places of darkness -- Wherein have they found PEACE - wherein have they found freedom? I say - they have found not the freedom which I offer them - neither have they found Peace ---

While I say: "Come and follow Me"- they offer up their platitudes, their rigamaroles - and they put their fingers in their ears that they hear not Mine Voice -- <u>Mine</u> <u>timing</u> <u>is</u> <u>correct</u> - for I say - when they listen unto Me I shall give unto them that which shall profit them -- They shall know - and know that they know - they shall not despair - for I shall sustain them -- They shall be as ones lifted up - for I shall lift them up -- Forget not that I AM HE which is SENT for to lift them up ---

I say - behold ye the Hand of God move - let it MOVE - and rejoice that it is now come that men might see and know -- FOR THIS AM I COME!

Forget not that this is the day of awakening - the day of CHANGE, the day long foretold -- So rejoice! Rejoice! And be glad!!

Forget not that there are ones now come in flesh to be Mine servants even as thou - and they shall <u>be</u> as ones (they shall not betray themself) and they shall do that which I give unto them to do with a glad heart -- They shall rejoice in Mine service - and they shall be blest for serving and not one shall go without his just reward - for I shall reward him according unto his service - his capacity to receive -- So be it and Selah

Recorded by Sister Thedra

This Day Shall Bear Fruit

Pete Conrad & Allen Bean on the Moon--

Blest be this day -- And I say unto thee this day shall bear fruit -- So be it it shall be as none other - for it shall be sweet and it shall be profitable unto all men -- For this is the day for which men have waited Knowing not that it is NOW COME - they wait and wait - yet I say: THIS IS THE DAY for which they have waited---

Now MEN shall walk the hiways and byways - knowing they are not alone - that they are wanderers on the periphery of the Universe - and they shall be as the wanderers for a time - for the time is not yet come when they knoweth the fullness of this day - for the fullness is yet not apparent unto them -- They say <u>this</u> - they say <u>that</u> - they are opinionated and they know not that the way is opened for them to become free - from the bonds of Earth - and the attraction of the Moon. I say they shall become free - even to go unto the planets of the System.

Yet for this they have not prepared themself -- I say: "Prepare thyself that ye break thy bonds!"-- Yet man shall become his brother's protector - "his brother's keeper" - his BROTHER!! - for he shall first learn that ALL are <u>brothers</u> - that all are <u>one</u> indeed!

Yet all are not of the same <u>order</u> - all are not of the same blood/ same flesh - while All are of the WHOLE -- Fear not - for "This Day Shall Bear Fruit" - I say: "THIS DAY SHALL BEAR FRUIT "---

So be it I have a hand in this -- Note well that which I say - for the day cometh when man shall soar the heights without the cumbersome gadgets which are <u>now</u> his-- He shall go out as the bird - free from any cumbersome gadgets -- I speak as One which <u>Knows</u> - for I am not asleep - I am not among the dead which sleepeth in darkness -- I KNOW - I am HE WHICH IS SENT THAT THIS DAY BEAR FRUIT.

It cometh swiftly when one shall take flight - and he shall be as one prepared - and he shall enter into a place where no Earthling hast ever been - and wherein he shall see wonders never before beheld by man of Earth -- I say <u>he</u> shall be as one <u>sent</u> for to see and to learn-- Yet many shall claim for themself such credit - and it shall be unto their own undoing ---

While "he" which is sent shall walk quietly and gently/ humbly amongst his fellowmen until his work be done - and he shall leave his report/ his findings for man's benefit and they shall profit thereby -- I say: beware of the braggards for they are wont to know - they are the ones unprepared to enter into the "Secret Places"-- I say unto thee: No man shall enter into the Holy of Holies unprepared --So be it and Selah

The Purpose

Sori Sori -- Be ye as one blest this day - for I come that ye be blest -- Let it be - as this is the day spoken of - and for this do I speak unto thee Now ye shall be as one which hast come unto this place for <u>the purpose</u> of lifting up the fallen -- I say ye shall first hold up thy own head and lift up thine eyes - that ye see that which goes on within the realms of Light - that which is not revealed unto the uninitiated -- Ye shall be as one <u>prepared</u> to go into the place wherein I shall lead thee -- Ye shall be as one on whose shoulders rests <u>great</u> responsibility - for I shall give unto thee in <u>Greater</u> measure ---

Bless thyself to be as one prepared - for I say unto thee: Great things are in store for thee -- Bless thyself and be ye as one prepared to bless others as I have blest thee -- Hear ye that which I say unto thee - and ye shall not fail neither shall ye fall ---

Recorded by Sister Thedra

The Greater & Lesser Councils

Sori Sori -- I come unto thee as One from out the Inner Temple wherein there are many which sit in council for the benefit of ALL ---

This Council is the Great and Grand Council wherein sit the ones which know that which shall be done -- For this are they able to direct the lesser Schools ---

Now I say unto thee: The School of Melchizedek is the School unto which We direct the workers which <u>would be</u> the Wayshowers - the workers which have devoted their lives their energy unto the enlightenment of the Earth and Her children ---

I say - the WORKERS which have given of themself are the ones which now sit in Council wherein there are ones which have the responsibility of siboring the few which <u>would</u> <u>be</u> the Wayshowers -- I call unto thee this day: Bring forth the ones which <u>would</u> <u>be</u> the wayshowers - and We will give unto them as they are prepared to receive -- For this have We prepared thee - that ye be as one prepared for the next part - the <u>Greater</u> <u>Part</u> -- Let it be said that when one comes into this Council Chamber he <u>IS</u> prepared for the work at hand -- So be it that I now speak unto thee that ye be prepared to enter in ---

Behold ye the Hand of <u>God</u> - for it moveth swiftly!

Be ye as one blest - for I bless thee with My Presence --

Recorded by Sister Thedra

Mother Eternal

Be ye blest and give unto them this Mine Word - and give unto them as I give unto thee - for before thou wast I was - I am - and I shall ever be thy <u>Mother</u> <u>Eternal</u> -- I speak unto thee of the Inner Temple - wherein I AM - wherein I abide - for within the Inner Temple ye shall come to know ME as I AM ---

Be ye as one prepared to come within the place of Mine abode - wherein ye shall know peace - and LOVE as I know -- Forget not that there rests upon thy shoulders great responsibility - for thou hast now come into the place wherein there are ones which await thy preparation for thy next part -- They have sibored thee and attended thee with Love and patience - and with profound Wisdom ---

I say - They await thy appearance within the Great Council Chambers wherein They hold forth -- By THEIR GRACE shall ye be prepared to enter in -- By thy own application and effort shall they be rewarded---

Put not thine foot in a hole - Place thine hand in Mine and I shall put thy foot on solid ground where in is no pitfall -- Place thine hand in Mine and I shall lift thee upon higher ground -- Come - Come - and we shall sup together and rejoice -- So be it and Selah ---

I bring with Me the Angelic Host that ye be prepared for the "Greater Part" -- So be it I see thee as thou art - not as thou dost appear unto mortals - for mortal eyes see not as I see - I see thee as THOU ART -- Envision Me as I AM - so be it we shall know each other as we are One - ONE I say -- Praise ye the Name of Solen Aum Solen - and be ye as one with Me for I am One with HIM --

So be it and Selah --

Recorded by Sister Thedra

Today's Exam: - BEATITUDE - - ATTITUDE

BEATITUDE: - "Supreme Blessedness - Exalted Happiness -- Any of the Declarations of Blessedness pronounced by Jesus* in the Sermon on the Mount"

ATTITUDE: - "Manner - Disposition - Feeling - Position with regard to a person or Thing - - Tendency or Orientation esp. of the Mind"

(Definitions from Random House Dict.)

* **Sananda**

* * * * * *

"Bless thyself . . Bless thyself as ye would that I bless thee" "Ye shall become that for which ye prepare thyself" - - Sananda

Ref: Temple Teachings Sananda & S.K.

* * * * * *

What is MY attitude?

Have I blest myself this day?

Or have I expected the LORD to do it for me?

What do I expect to become?

Have I been true to myself today?

Am I that which I profess to be?

Do I follow the LORD GOD - or another?

Do I believe that which HE SAYS?

Is my faith sufficient to go all the way with HIM?

Am I fearful of being rejected?

Am I afraid of failure?

Sickness?

Loneliness?

Poverty?

Can I forsake all to follow THE LORD OF LORDS?

Can I stand alone when the tempest rages?

WHAT IS MY ATTITUDE - toward conditions?

What are my leg irons that hold me bound?

Do I presume to know the GREAT DIVINE PLAN for me - or my fellow men? Shall I presume to tell the LORD GOD what is best for us?

Have I held on to the old - refusing the new?

Have I been blinded by orthodoxy and tradition?

Have I defended TRUTH and JUSTICE at all times?

Have I become a bigot in my conceit?

Have I been proud of my humility?

Have I refused the "GOLDEN KEY" SO GRACIOUSLY offered?

Have I been grateful for all opportunities to LEARN?

Have I grown OLD in my conceit and IGNORANCE?

Have I reap't that which I have sown without rebellion - and in DIGNITY?

Have I attempted to escape this day - while reaching for tomorrow?

What <u>IS</u> MY ATTITUDE?

Personal from Sister Thedra

I am the Law

Sori Sori -- Say unto them in Mine name - that I am He which hast come that there be Light -- While they are as ones walking blindly - I say they shall be made to see - for they shall come to know that I AM COME - that I AM He which is Sent that they be brot out of bondage.

Now ye shall give unto them this Word - and they shall be wise indeed to accept it - for it is the Word of the Law - which I AM ---

I say: I AM THE LAW - and it is not to be set aside ---

Fear not - for I have said I shall cover thee -- I shall do that which I will - and ye shall find Peace within Me - for I am that which ye seek. SEEK and ye shall find - for I am He which is come that ye have Light. So be it that there is no other way unto the "Father's House" -- Let it suffice thee that I Know the Way - and I shall lead safely and surely -- I shall bring thee <u>Home</u> -- So be it and Selah ---

Say unto them - they shall be as ones prepared for to receive ME - and I shall remember them in the time of stress -- So be it and Selah

Forget not that I stand on the High Holy Mount as One which Knows the Way into the place wherein ALL things are known -- So be it that I stand as One prepared to assist thee in thy ascent - and I am One Sent that ye have the assistance so necessary - for there are many pitfalls -- Yet I have said: "Follow Ye Me" and no harm shall come nigh unto thee - nothing shall say unto thee - Stay! for this have I given unto thee passport into the Secret Place of the Most High ---

Forget not there is no other way - save thru ME ---

I AM THE LIGHT - TRUTH and THE WAY -- So be it and Selah

Recorded by Sister Thedra

These Shall Be Given the Power

Sori Sori -- Be ye as the hand of Me and record that which I say unto thee - that they too might know that which I say - for it shall be for the Good of All -- While there are many which shall deny Me - and Mine Word - there are many which shall heed the Word - and these I shall bless - and make known unto them greater things -- For the time is at hand when man shall bless the day when they accept the Word -- I say Blest shall they be which receive unto themself the WORD ---

Let it be known that I AM COME that the WORD be made manifest upon the Earth -- There is but few which have the power which shall be given unto them which I shall raise up - for these shall be given the power and the authority to do the things which I do - for they shall be like unto Mine hands and Mine feet - and they shall be swift to do that which I give unto them to do -- They shall go where I go and do that which I do - and they shall be as ones prepared to go all the way with Me - and they shall receive their inheritance even as I have received Mine -- So be it that I say <u>this day</u>: Be ye blest to receive Me and of Me for this have I spoken unto thee -- By the power and authority invested within Me - I say: It is now come when I shall give unto thee as I have received - and it is for this that I say: "Come follow Me and I shall give unto thee as ye have not received"- these are Mine gifts unto thee -- For this day have I kept watch - for this day have I kept Watch! For "<u>This Day</u>" have I KEPT WATCH ---

Now that it is come - I shall call forth the ones which have the mind to follow Me - and I shall endow unto them that which I have been fortuned -- I shall give unto them as I have received of Mine Father Which hast Sent Me -- I say unto thee: Behold in Me the Light which I AM -- So be it I AM the LIGHT - the WAY -- So be it and Selah

Recorded by Sister Thedra

They Reject the Strait and Narrow Way

Sori Sori -- Behold ye the hand of God move - it moveth by the Will of Him which is Sent -- He which is come - cometh thru the Will of the Father which hast Sent Me -- So be it I am the Son Sent of Him - that His Will be done on Earth as it is in "Heaven"-- So let it be as He hast Willed it ---

For this I now say unto thee: See - SEE the hand of God move - for I say unto thee - there is a plan - a divine plan - and none shall say Me nay!

I bring with Me a plan - I seek out them which are prepared to go all the way with Me - and I give unto them as they are prepared to receive -- Yet I say - few have come forth as prepared to receive the fullness of the plan -- I see them faint and fall by the way - I hear them cry and plead - yet they have not been unto themself true - they ask for the blessings of man - yet they weary of Mine Sayings - and they give unto themself credit for being wise --

They ask for the frills and the glitter while they reject the strait and narrow way which I would show them -- I have walked the Earth with bare feet and a contrite heart in the simplicity of a disciple/ adept/ Master/ yet they ask for the glitter - signs - wonders -- While I say: "Come unto Me empty handed - bare of heart - with all thy being serve Me - Me only - follow ye Me and I shall reveal unto thee many things"- yet they weary - they seek comfort - ease - and reject that which I proffer them in LOVE and Wisdom -- So be it I Know them and their needs -- I Know that which I have for them - and it shall profit them to receive the Gifts I have kept for them -- So be it they far exceed all the trash which they might accumulate - <u>All</u> <u>Earth's</u> <u>Riches</u>!! I say I am not alone in this - Great is the Army - Great is the Host - for they gather from All the Universe that this day bring forth Great Light ---

I tell thee of a Surety - the day cometh when All the Sons of God shall Sing together as of long ago -- They shall rejoice - for the day cometh swiftly when they shall be glorified before the Throne of The Most High Living God Solen Aum Solen -- Praise ye His Name and let it be as He hast Willed it ---

Praise ye the Lord of Lords for He is Come -- Make way for the Lord is Come - praise - Praise - PRAISE ye The God of ALL - Solen Aum Solen --

Recorded by Sister Thedra

The Hour of Resurrection

Sori Sori -- For this day let it be given unto thee this Word which shall be given unto them which await the hour of their resurrection - I say: "For them which await the hour of their resurrection"---

Now let it be known that the hour draws nigh when they shall be resurrected - and they shall step forth from the body of dense flesh - into the body of pure Light - wherein they shall be One with the Light and of the Light - Then they shall go forth as ones free from flesh - from the gravitation of Earth - and they shall have NO bounds for nothing shall bind them ---

It is now come when many shall know this freedom even as I -- For this have I said: "Come Follow Me" -- For this have I said: "Ye shall go where I go"-- And unto them which COME UNTO ME - I shall give unto them as I to have received -- So be it and Selah ---

I Am Come that ALL might be free - yet few choose ME and My Way - yet it is the ONLY way -- So be it and Selah ---

I have sent forth Mine Servants - Mine Emissaries - Mine Messengers by the score - yet they have been unacceptable unto the masses -- I say unto thee: The masses are the poor of spirit - they are impoverished - they know not that I Am <u>Come</u> - that I AM HE which is Sent of Mine Father -- Yet I cry aloud - COME -- I speak from the Mountain top - I speak from the valley - I call unto them in a loud Voice I say: LOOK - SEE!! - yet they turn their face from Me -- They are affrighted and they run after <u>man</u> and his opinions --

They question the soothsayers and they question the dead - and fear in their questioning -- They seek in dark places for the answers -- "The Signs of the Times" frighten them - yet I say the "HANDWRITING ON THE WALL" hast been interpreted in the Scripts of Old -- Look - See! and understand that this is the end of the age - the beginning of the age --

This is the time when I shall go forth. as the Reaper -- This is the day when I shall gather in the harvest of the old - and I shall plant anew I say I shall plant anew -- I shall set up My Kingdom and I shall draw forth Water from the Rock -- I shall draw forth Substance from the Unseen - and I shall plant Mine Staff/ Mine Standard upon the hill top and no man shall say Me nay! for I shall reign as Lord God over Mine Kingdom - and none shall stay Mine hand - for I have been given the Authority and the POWER by the Father of ALL - which hast Sent Me forth that this mighty Work be done on Earth as it is in Heaven -- So be it and Selah ---

I Am He - I AM HE - I AM HE which is COME --

So be it and Selah

Recorded by Sister Thedra

Bear Ye Witness

Bear ye witness of Me and give unto them this Mine Word - for it shall profit them to hear and heed that which I say - for the time is come when I shall speak out - and it shall be for the Good of All ---

Be ye as Mine hand made manifest unto them - and record for them this Mine Word - that they might have it - for this shall ye be blest -- Now they shall return unto their altars and make for themself graven images - and put their money in their tills - and say their sayings with fervor - yet it shall make them no more prepared -- They shall sing their hymns and shout their praise - yet this is not enuf -- I say: This is NOT SUFFICIENT -- They shall do that which the Father Wills - they shall bless themself by obedience unto the law --

They shall bless others by their obedience - for it follows as the night the day: -- First ye shall bless thyself - love thy Life - for it is a Gift which no man giveth - the Gift the Father hast bestowed upon thee.- Given unto thee thru His Love and Mercy - that ye might Know Him - for this I come -- Bless thyself by obedience unto the LAW -- Forget not that the LAW is exact - it is no respecter of persons - and shows no favorites --

Therefore I say unto thee - unto All - Follow in the "Way" set before thee - and ye shall not fall - neither shall ye die - for I say: Ye shall not taste of death - for death shall have no power over thee -- Fear not - for I say death shall not touch thee -- It hast been said that ye shall step forth from thy physical form of flesh into thy body of Light Substance - which is eternal and knows no death - no darkness -- I say: Death shall not touch thee - for it shall be overcome and be as nothing --

First ye shall seek the Light and it shall not be hidden from thee -- So be it and Selah ---

Hast it not been given unto thee to come from out the Light wherein thou hadst thy beginning? Hast it not been said - ye shall return unto thy Source?

So let it be as The Father hast Willed-

So shall it be -- Amen and Selah

Recorded by Sister Thedra

TRANSITION

Sori Sori -- For this day let it be understood that the time comes swiftly when each one shall forfeit the physical form - and he shall take up another - for this is the law --The law is just and fails not - for it is the plan from the beginning - let it be -- And it behooves Me to say that none escapes the law -- Yet I say: When the form which is the earthly form μ comes to its duration - its end - it shall return unto its Source -- And then one shall take its place - the one of finer Substance and of Greater intensity -- Of the Light shall these bodies be made - Wherein is it said: "Ye go from Glory to Glory?" it is so -- So be it and Selah -- Now ye shall remember that which is said - "Ye go from Glory to Glory"---

Be it So - So shall it ever be -- For this has it been said - "Prepare thyself for the Greater Part"- for this is the day of fulfillment -- I say ye shall go forth as one prepared -- So be it and Selah

Recorded by Sister Thedra

In the Time of Stress

Say unto them: There shall be great stress - and they shall be as ones prepared for that which shall come upon them -- They shall stand firm and waver not - for they shall be tried as by fire -- Yet it is said that neither the fire nor wind shall stay them -- So be it that I am come that they be strengthened in their weak parts -- So be it and Selah --

For this do I say: "Come follow Me and I shall give unto thee as ye are prepared to receive"-- Now I say: "Be ye as ones prepared for the GREATER PART"- for it is <u>now</u> time that ye come out of darkness and follow the Light which I AM ---

By Mine own hand shall I lead thee - and by Mine own strength shall I sustain thee -- Know ye that I shall do that which I have said I will do - for I am not to be turned aside - for I am come that there be LIGHT -- So let it be ---

Thy way is not My way - thy light is not sufficient -- I come that ye might have Greater Light - that ye might be sufficient unto thyself -- So be it I am Sent of Mine Father that ye be brot out of darkness -- So be it and Selah

Let the winds blow - let them blow - for nothing shall be unto thee a detriment - for I am come that ye be blest -- So shall it be -- Let it Be

Recorded by Sister Thedra

The Kingdom of God

Sori Sori -- Mine time hast come when I shall go forth as the King of Kings -- I shall hold forth as the King and I shall set up Mine Kingdom and none shall overthrow it - for it shall be built upon a <u>Solid</u> Foundation - and it shall not fall -- So be it and Selah ---

For this have I come - that it be made manifest on the Earth as it is in <u>Heaven</u> -- So be it and Selah --

While I say - it is now come when I shall set up Mine Kingdom - I too say - that Mine Kingdom is not of the Earth -- Hast it not been said that "Mine Kingdom is not of the Earth"- it is so - it is of the Father's Realm which hast Sent Me -- Therefore I say: "Come ye - follow where I lead thee and I shall make thee one of Mine Kingdom - I shall give unto thee that which is sufficient unto thee - I shall give unto thee that which is needful - and be unto thee all that the Father would have Me be"-- So let it be as the Father Wills it -- I have said that I Am He which is Sent that His Kingdom be established - and it is so ---

Now ye shall go forward knowing that which I say - and ye shall walk with Me and talk with Me -- Ye shall do that which I give unto thee to do -- So be it and Selah

I AM COME - I AM COME that ALL might have Light -- Yet I say: Few have seen - few have heard - many wait - many fail - many cry out - while I say: COME UNTO ME and be made WHOLE ---

So shall they wait and cry - for they shall be as ones <u>prepared</u> to enter into the Kingdom of Heaven --

So be it the LAW -

Recorded by Sister Thedra

Gold from the Crucible

Sori Sori -- Mighty is the hand of God -- Swift is the hand of the Almighty <u>One</u> ---

I am come that ye see the hand move in all its swiftness and surety for with swiftness and surety it moveth - It passeth over the Earth as the Winged Eagle -- It passeth over the Seas and the land as the mighty fortress - and it bringeth peace unto the initiated -- Yet unto the uninitiated it might bring great fear and foreboding - for its power is felt by the uninitiated - and knowing not that which is felt - they fear - Yet I say unto thee - fear not - for I am come that this day be fulfilled.

I am come that <u>this</u> <u>day</u> be the fulfillment of all past ages -- So be it <u>this</u> <u>day</u> shall bring forth the Gold from the Crucible in its radiant purity - and nothing shall contaminate it - neither shall it be destroyed any more -- It shall be as nothing known unto man in ages past -- I am come that man be liberated from his bondage ---

I am Come! I AM COME! I AM COME!

WATCH! SEE! KNOW! - for this Am I COME -

Recorded by Sister Thedra

The Christ Child
The Way

Sori Sori -- Hear ye! Hear ye! - and take note - for I Am He which is Sent that ALL men might hear - heed and be blest ---

I come this day that the Voice be heard in the wilderness --

I come that it be made manifest in the Earth ---

I come that it be done as the Father hast willed it - So be it and Selah

Behold ye the Light which I AM -- Behold ye the Way I point -- Walk ye in the Way I set before thee ---

Behold ye the Work which I do - be ye as part of the Work -- Put thy hand in Mine - and I shall lead thee in ways new unto thee -- Fear not for I am thy Shield and thy Buckler -- I AM the WAY - TRUTH - LIFE - LIGHT -- I Am He which has given of Mineself that ye might have Light - that ye want not ---

Now I say: Behold ye the Light which I AM --- Behold ye the Way which I AM -- Behold ye the Life which I AM ---

Behold ye the Door which I AM - for I AM the DOOR thru which ye pass into the Holy of Holies -- So be it said unto thee: COME! - be ye as one prepared to enter into the "Kingdom of Heaven" - for therein ye shall find thine name written in the Book of Life -- I say Come - be ye as one prepared to enter in - and therein ye shall find thy name written in the Book of Life ---

Hear ye Me and walk as I -- Walk with Me -- Sing ye the paeans of PRAISE - for unto thee is given a Child -- I say: "Unto thee is given a Child" - and ye shall nourish and bring to maturity this Child - for it is the Gift from on High -- The Christ Child is this day born within thee. Behold in Him the Light which I AM ---

Behold in Him the Way - the Door -- The entrance is for the most part obscure - yet I say: Follow ye Me and I shall lead thee --

Fear not - hold fast and ye shall not fail --

Recorded by Sister Thedra

Light (Freedom) vs Darkness (Bondage)

Be ye as one blest this day - and give unto them this Word - and it shall profit them to receive it - for they shall bless themself to receive it for it is Mine -- And none shall put their hand to Mine mouth - for I shall speak out - and they shall come to know the true from the false! I say the liars shall be as the <u>liars</u> and the true shall remain the TRUE servants of Mine Father which hast sent Me -- For many a true prophet hast been martyred and given the fortune to lose his vehicle - while they now sit at the feet of their false prophets - and listen unto the foolish prattle of the unknowing one ---

I say they sit at the feet of their false prophets and ask of the <u>liars</u> that which they (the <u>liars</u>) know not!

They seek in dark places for information concerning the dark places concerning their desires - wants -- They are as the vermin on the heads of the innocent -- They know the torment - yet they know not the cause. They know not that they have brot about their own torment ---

I say unto them which ask of the liars (the familiar spirits) that they are giving of their spirit - of their strength - that they might have voice that they might be bound unto them - as familiar spirits ---

Now I say they shall be as ones tormented - for their time is come. I say unto "them": Give not the "dead" power over thee - give the liars no voice - heed them not! for they but lead thee into the pit! They have not the Light! -- They are bound in darkness and the truth is not in them I say!! -- HEAR YE ME! And be no part of their darkness! for they would drag thee down into the pit of darkness wherein they are ---

Thy strength is not sufficient - thy wisdom is not sufficient - - ye shall stand upon the ROCK and give unto Me credit for knowing that which I say - for I AM the LIGHT - TRUTH - THE WAY - and I Am come that ye be brot out of darkness ---

So be it I Am Sent of The Father -- Adore Him - Praise ye Him - and bless thyself in the doing! So be it I am come that ye be blest --

Recorded by Sister Thedra

Surely Love & Mercy Shall Prevail

Sori Sori -- This I would say unto thee: Be ye as one prepared for that which I shall give unto thee - and it shall be for the good of all -- And they shall bear witness of that which I say - for it shall be for them which have a mind to follow Me -- And unto <u>them</u> I say: Heed Mine Word for it is for <u>thee</u> -- And it shall behoove them to heed well <u>the Word</u> - for it is now come when they shall ponder the Word which I have given unto <u>them</u> - and for this do I now remind them again -- And again I find it expedient to say that I am the Way thru which they enter into the Holy of Holies - for it is the plan given of Mine Father which hast Sent ME -- None other hast He given Mine part - this part which He hast allotted unto Me ---

While they seek the answers of the dead - they are filled with fear - and they are as ones walking with the "dead" -- While they are as ones walking with the "dead" they give of themself unto them which draw from them their energy - strength and life force -- They shall turn from their <u>own</u> way and seek the Light which I AM -- They shall no longer credit Me with the words of the liars and falsifiers - for they put words into Mine mouth which I spew out!

I say I SPEW them OUT OF MINE MOUTH! Hear ye then and be ye forewarned!

I SAY: I shall not put Mine hand upon them to stay their misery - until they seek the Truth - the Light!!

I am not of them - I am not with them - they deceive themself -- Yet I say - be ye not deceived ---

I am come that ye have Light -- I now speak that ye be spared a pitfall far worse than "death" - for it is Mine part to warn thee - thine part to heed Mine Word ---

Listen! Heed - and be ye as one prepared to receive Me -- First ye shall receive Mine Servant - Mine Word - then I shall place Mine hand upon thee - and ye shall know the true from the false!

So let it be

Recorded by Sister Thedra

The Way of Initiation

Hail! Hail! unto them that enter into the Holy of Holies-- Hail! Hail! unto the Victor!

Blest are they that overcome -- Blest are they that come into the place wherein I am ---

Blest are they that receive as I have received -- I say - Hail! Hail! unto the Victor!

By Mine own hand shall I crown him the <u>Victor</u> -- By Mine own hand shall I bless him -- By Mine own hand shall I give unto him as I have received of Mine Father---

For it is given unto Me the authority and power to give as I have received -- So shall I give unto them which are prepared as I was prepared -- So be it and Selah ---

Let it be known that there is no other way into the secret place of the Most High Living God save by Me -- And I am aware of thy preparation and thy part - thy success - thy failures - thy wants - thy sacrifices - thy will - thy time -- And it is now come when one shall come unto thee - and he shall give unto thee a part which shall be for the good of all -- And it shall be given unto them - and they shall accept in the name of the Father - Son and Mighty Council -- I say: "The Mighty Council"- for it is thru the Council that ye receive such instructions as shall profit thee -- While there are ones which <u>would</u> give unto thee of their own parts (the poor part from the poor in spirit) these are not of the Light - and know not the Light - neither have they found their way --

Now these would hold in bondage them which ask of them - which give of themself that they (the earth-bound spirit – T.) have strength - for they feed upon the strength of them which listen and obey -- I say they are parasites -- Too I say: Let it cease -- Give not of thyself to the parasites - let it cease! Be ye as ones free from them -- It is said that thy wisdom is not sufficient - neither thy strength - for thou hast not as yet gained the summit -- The way is steep and the climb is strenuous - slip not -- I have spoken of the pitfalls - I have spoken of the temptations - the failures - of thy weakness -- I have too spoken of the joy of success, of the Ascent to the Mountain top - the Glories of the ascent - the overcoming -- And therein is the strength - the power - the joy - for all other is as nothing --

I have put before thee all that ye shall have need of -- I have placed within thy hands the LAWS - the / Light is before thee - I say SEE IT! See it and be ye not so foolish as to reject it - for thy waiting should be sad and hard indeed -- So be it ye shall heed Mine Word and be glad - For this have I spoken out this day - for one shall hear - and one shall not hear -- And unto the one that hears I say COME -- Unto the one which does not hear I say: Pass ye not in for thou hast not prepared thyself for to enter in - so be it the LAW! I am come that there be Light! SEE IT and hear ye Me - and be ye BLEST this day --

I am Not to Be Turned Aside

Sori Sori -- Let this be recorded that they might have it - that they come to know that which I do -- And these shall I give unto sufficiently -- I shall give unto them that which shall sustain them and they shall know no sorrow -- These I shall deliver out of bondage - and these shall know no death -- While I say unto thee - ye shall give unto them these Words. I say ye shall not trespass upon their free will -- Let it suffice that they have Mine Word - and they shall heed it or reject it -- And unto them which reject it I say: Pity is thy plight - for thou hast chosen the way of bondage and darkness ---

Be ye as one free to choose which way ye go -- Be ye blest to choose the Way I place before thee - for the Way I show thee is strait and narrow – the / (light T.)-- So be it that I go before thee that ye find thy way safely and without sorrow -- For this have I told thee of the pitfalls Place thy hand in Mine and I shall lead thee safely -- Unto them which use the name "Sananda" falsely - I will place them before the scales of Justice - and they shall be brot to account - and justice shall prevail -- For this I have provided that justice prevail - for this have I provided that ye be not bound by the false ones which would trip thee up -- Now I say unto them which have set up their <u>OWN</u> altars: "Be ye as ones prepared for that which thou hast set into motion - for it shall be visited upon thee - and ye shall see the folly of thy own vanity - thy own foolishness"---

So be ye not as the "foolish virgins" - for I am not of a mind to give unto the foolish Mine Oil -- I give unto Mine own - therefore I say: "Come ye forth - follow ye Me"- and give no ear unto the liars which would - and do - design to trip them up and hold thee bound in the web of illusion -- I have spoken - it hast been recorded for thee - and I am not finished -- I have said they shall hear Me - and no man shall shut Mine mouth - for I am not to be turned out or put aside -- Now I say unto the ones which follow Me: Be ye not turned aside by their deceit, their flattery - their dubious messages and their honeyed tongue - for it is the way of the dragon - in which he holds them bound -- Be ye no part of them -- Walk ye in the Light which I AM - and I shall remember thee all the days of thy life ---

So be it that I am not deceived -- I am not lured by their wishes - their pitiful petitions - their places of iniquity -- I say I am not lured into their false temples - therefore I say unto thee: Enter not! lest ye put thy foot into a hole -- Forfeit not thy freedom - for I say ye shall be alert and wise as the serpent and silent as the sphinx -- So let it profit thee

Recorded by Sister Thedra

The Reward of Obedience

Sori Sori -- For this day let it go on record - that one shall go from the place wherein I am - and he shall find thee and he shall bring thee hence and for this shall ye be prepared -- He shall find thee by thy light - and ye shall be glad that ye have prepared thyself for to receive him ---

Now let it be given unto them which are of a mind to receive that which hast been recorded - and they shall know that which I have said.

It shall be recorded as it is said - and it shall be for the good of all that it be recorded as it is spoken -- Fear not that which they say or do, that which they shall do - for it is thy part to do that which I give unto thee to do -- It matters not that which "they" do - let not thy foot slip - let NOT THY FOOT SLIP! - FEAR NOT ---

For this do I say: Follow ye Me - and ye shall not fail -- For this do I give unto thee the Word - that they too might know - that they too might be free to go where I go -- Let it be -- As they are prepared so shall they receive - for it is the LAW ---

Recorded by Sister Thedra

What is the Plan

Be ye as one blest this day - and give unto them this Mine Word - and it shall suffice them -- There shall be a a great light amongst them - and they shall see and know that there is a plan - and it shall be carried forth in <u>Great</u> <u>Speed</u> - for the time is now come when one shall go forth as one prepared to give of himself that the plan be brot into its fullness -- The plan is the fulfillment of the Word - the fulfillment of All that hast been said ---

The plan is the establishment of God's Kingdom on Earth and the fulfillment of the design thereof -- So be it and Selah -- Now ye shall take up thy Shield and Buckler and go forth as one prepared -- So be it that I shall give unto thee as thou art prepared to receive -- So be it and Selah ---

Recorded by Sister Thedra

The Place is Prepared

Sori Sori -- For this day - let it be said that one shall give unto thee a part for the ones which hast gone this far with thee - and he shall be as one which hast received the fullness of his inheritance even as I -- I bless him and he blesses me - even as we bless thee - for it is for this that we will to bring unto thee the blessings which we are so lovingly sharing -- I say we are sharing with thee our blessing which we have received of the Mighty Council - for in one body We sit as with one hand - one mind --

We move and counsel thee as <u>One</u> for it is not given unto us to divide ourself - we are of ONE mind -- Therefore I say unto thee which are of a mind to receive of me: Let the mind which is in ME be the mind which is in thee - for I am of a mind to bring thee out of bondage -- Hear ye me in this for I am come that YE be of the mind to be delivered out ---

While I find it expedient to pluck them out one at a time I say - I shall pluck them out as they are prepared - for I shall send one which is prepared to receive them - and as they are prepared so shall they <u>be</u> received into the place prepared -- So let it be as they are prepared - for each unto his own - in his own time -- For this have I spoken that each might know the law and prepare himself to receive the fullness of his inheritance - that he might be received within his Father's House from whence he went forth -- So be it and Selah ---

Forget not that the Council sits in Council for the good of all - yet there are ones which have not lifted a finger - they sit as ones made of clay - <u>unanimated</u> by Spirit - they sit as ones <u>dead</u> - and are they not the living dead without the Spirit? <u>I</u> <u>say</u> they are the living dead - they eat and spawn - yet they bring forth not heirs unto everlasting life - that the Father's Kingdom be glorified -- So be it I shall go forth and gather up Mine own - and I shall clear away the debris and make way for a new race of men which shall walk as <u>man</u> glorified of the Father -- And His Kingdom shall be like unto none other which hast been upon the Earth.-

I say unto thee come out from amongst them and be ye as one prepared to go where I go - for I have prepared a place wherein ye may be prepared for the Greater part ---

I say - <u>Glorious</u> is the place which I have prepared for thee -- Build ye greater mansions and greater shall be thine reward -- I bless thee with Mine presence - and the Word is recorded for them which hast followed thru unto this point -- Let it be for them and withhold it from them which hast not gone thus far -- So shall ye be blest ---

Recorded by Sister Thedra

The Ordained Priests & Priestesses

Sori Sori -- Hast it not been said that one shall come unto thee for to give unto thee a part which shall bless thee - and all which shall ask for to receive of him -- So be it he is come - receive him in the name of the Father and the Son which he is -- So be it and Selah ---

For this do I speak out this day that all might be blest -- And all which accept mine word shall be blest as I have been blest by the Father which hast sent me ---

Now it is come when I might come as one prepared to touch thee - guide and counsel thee -- As there are many which are seeking the Light I come unto thee at this time that they might come to know that which we have in store for them -- Yet it is said "They shall seek the Light first"- and it shall not be hidden from them - for this day shall bear fruit and the generations yet unborn shall at thereof -- So be it and Selah --

Wherefore hast thou contributed unto the next generation - and wherein hast thou served the Lord thy God with all thy strength? For it is for thy own sake that I remind thee of thy short comings and thy idleness -- There are many which seek the Light this day - art thou prepared to lead them? Wherefore then art thou qualified to be as censor unto the ones which have been called and ordained to speak for the Council and the Lord of Lords? Wherein hast thou been given the authority to criticize or to blame? Wherein hast thou been taught that which the priest or priestess hast been taught?

I say thou shall learn from the priest and priestess which hast been taught and ordained - by the authority which is given unto thee of the Mighty Council and the Father which hast set it apart -- Be ye not so foolish as to set thy foot against one of mine which I have called and appointed - for they are <u>mine</u> - and inasmuch as they are <u>mine</u> - thou hast done it unto ME -- So be it and Selah ---

Look! See! and KNOW! Be ye as the wise - and the fools shall prattle on - and mine servants shall be as ones which have their lamps trimmed and burning - while the fools shall be as the "foolish Virgins"- without oil -- And darkness shall overtake them and they shall not find their way into the place wherein I am -- So be it that I am prepared to give unto each as he is prepared to receive -- So be it and Selah ---

Recorded by Sister Thedra

Choose Your Way Wisely

Sori Sori -- Let this be for the good of all - let it be given unto them which seek the Light - let it be given unto them which come unto thee seeking TRUTH - and unto them which are of a mind to follow in the way which I point -- I say - let them which ask for truth be given - for they shall find ---

Now it is come when there shall be many seeking the Light and they shall find - for this am I come unto thee for I am the Wayshower - I have pointed the way - and unto them which are of a mind to follow me I say come - come ye forth as one prepared -- Yet there is the way of darkness which beckons unto thee - ye shall choose which way ye shall go -- Too - I say - ye shall choose wisely for the choice is thine -- I say - be ye alert! And watchful! ---

Let not thy foot slip - place thy hand in mine and I shall lead the gently -- Be ye as one mindful of me - of thy footsteps - and of the pitfalls - hold ye fast! Be ye as one prepared to go all the way - for there is <u>great joy</u> for the one which goes all the way with me -- Let thine hand be firmly placed in mine and let thine feet be firm upon the way - and bless this day - that ye might be prepared for the days ahead -- So let it be for the good of all -- Hear ye me and consider well mine sayings ---

Be ye blest to receive me and of me -- So be it and Selah --

Recorded by Sister Thedra

A Sponsor

Sori Sori -- This day I would bring unto thee one which hast upon his head the Crown of the Sun - and he hast come as one from on high -- Thru the Great and Mighty Council of Sun Spa he comes -- So be it he is as one prepared to assist thee - he has within his hand the power to bless thee as he has been blest -- So be it that he hast been within the place wherein I am - and there is no place wherein he cannot go - for he hast <u>proven</u> himself -- He is ONE with ME - therefore he may go where I go - he may do that which I do - for he is one with me -- And for this is it proper that he be allowed to come unto thee for the purpose of assisting thee in the work at hand -- And let it be said - there is much to be done - and greater things than thou hast imaged - for it is said: This is the time of action - when they shall be alert and they shall cry out for light- and they shall be as ones prepared to receive it - for it shall not be hidden up from them ---

Now ye shall put thy pen unto the paper and record these his words and thereby bless thyself - for it is by thy own part that ye are blest -- While I say he shall bless thee as he hast been blest - I too say he has chosen to bless thee - thereby he is blest -- Now ye shall bless thyself by accepting him and his blessings - that others might be blest -- "This is the day of ACTION"- the day of participation when each shall have a part in the action which is "THE PLAN"---

They speak of a plan - yet they know not the plan - neither do they know their part - for they for the most part - hear but their own foolish prattle which is not theirs but that which hast been put into their mouth by another -- Few have the knowledge of the Council - or the working therein - I say - few know the working therein -- And it behooves me to say unto thee: There are ones come unto thee that ye might know - therefore I bring this one which wears the "Crown of the Sun" upon his head - and he shall give unto thee as he hast received of me -- So be it and Selah ---

Sori Sori-- I am he which hast come in the name of mine Father which is called Solen Aum Solen the ALL - the ONE -- Hear ye me and be ye as one blest - for this do I come unto thee ---

I am not alone in this - for a thousand times thousands are the numbers which stand with me - and for this do I say I am not alone -- I tell thee there are many times the number of thy Earth's population - which are with me that this work might encompass the Earth and her heavens round about -- I say unto thee - the Earth and her heavens shall be brot out of darkness - for this do we <u>now</u> make ourself known unto thee ---

I say: Praise ye THE LORD OF LORDS - THE HOST OF HOSTS. For HE shall do a mighty work and ye shall be as his servant - and as <u>His</u> shall ye be blest - for by thy service art thou blest - by thy light art thou found - by thy light shall thou be selected for thy part -- Fain would I tell thee of a part which thou couldst not partake of -- Fain would I call thee forth unprepared -- Fain would I give unto thee a plan which thou should not attain - the fulfillment thereof -- Put thine hand to the plow - and put thine head into the wind and move with the seasons - and it shall come to pass that one shall open up the Book of Life - and ye shall read therein the fullness of all things which are and have been. So be it that I am one prepared to sponsor thee - for I shall abide with thee - that ye be prepared to enter into the <u>Secret</u> <u>Place</u> of the Most High Living God -- So be it and Selah---

For this am I now come -- For this do I say unto thee - place thine hand to the plow - put thine head into the wind - and I shall be unto thee all that ye shall have need of -- Praise ye the Name of Solen Aum Solen for HE only is the ONE and the ALL ---

Praise ye Him forever and forever --

Recorded by Sister Thedra

Speaks of the Plan

Sori Sori -- This day I would say unto thee: Behold the <u>Glories</u> of the LORD - behold the way in which he works - for it is new unto thee -- Strange it is ---

Now ye shall see the wisdom therein - and ye shall know that thou art not alone ---

While I tell thee for a surety there are many which art nigh unto - and stand by - to assist thee - I say these are the ones which have attained the summit -- These are the ones which have risen - and are forever free from the gravitation of the Earth and the attraction of the Moon -- These are the ones which sit in council and prepare the way for thee -- These are the ones which hast given of themself without reserve that ye might find thy own way back unto the Father's House - So be it that I stand by as one of these - I am come that ye too find thy own way - yet it shall be thru thy own effort of obedience and service, service unto the Light - service unto them which seek the Light ---

Now ye shall give unto them as ye have received - and they shall walk upright and faithful unto the precepts and concepts which have been set forth in these parts which have been given unto them - in a plan which is from the beginning of the Earth - yea - even before the world was - the plan was ---

Now ye shall know there is a plan - and ye shall heed the law by obedience - and serve the Lord God with all thy heart and hand -- Speak only words of truth and wisdom - let not thy head rule thy heart - let not thy hand be turned to destruction -- Rather let thy head be given unto learning the greater things - thy heart to love - thy hands swift to lift up thy fellow man - the fallen which cry out for assistance -- Let them which suffer be comforted - let them which cry be comforted - let them which be dying be comforted - let them which are dumb speak - let them which are deaf hear - let them which are blind see - let them which are dead arise! Let them which are lame leap up and walk - let them which are poor arise and come forth and find the riches of mine Father's House ---

Let them come one and all - let them come forth and be blest -- Praise ye the Lord of Lords - praise ye the Lord God - for he is Lord of Lords - the King of Kings -- Let it be remembered that he is come - and ye shall sing a new song - for it is now come when ye shall sing praise unto the <u>new dawn</u> wherein man shall know him and be glad -- So be it that I am come that they might know - so shall this be - and ye shall be glad for thy part ---

Holy - Holy is the name of Solen Aum Solen - the Father of ALL - the Cause of our BEING -- So be it that I am glad for this day - for I have waited long for this time -- Let it be as the Father hast willed it.

Recorded by Sister Thedra

A Scattered People

Sori Sori -- For this day let it be known that I am come that there be light - and that there be peace amongst mine people -- So be it and Selah. For this do I sift and sort - and bring them together as one people. Yet I say they shall be as a scattered people - for I shall raise up a people which shall be of all nations of the Earth - and they shall have one mind

- which is to serve the Light - to serve the cause of Truth and Justice -- And they shall walk as one which hast mine hand upon him - for I shall direct and counsel him - as <u>one</u> <u>man</u> - for I shall be no respecter of race - nationality - neither shall I give unto them creeds and dogmas -- I shall give unto them the law - and they shall follow it - and they shall bow down unto no false god ---

They shall worship the Father - Cause of their being - and He shall give unto them as they are prepared to receive -- Now it is come when there shall rise up from the multitude one which is prepared to take great responsibility - and he shall lead a people which I shall bring out of bondage - and he shall know that which he is about -- He shall have within his hand the rod of power- and he shall have the authority to do that which is to do -- He shall bless all which choose to follow him - for he hast been chosen for this - his part - and he shall see it thru -- So be it I am at the post assigned unto me of mine Father - and this one shall serve under me the Lord of Lords - and I shall set up a Kingdom which no man shall overthrow ---

I say - no man shall overthrow MINE KINGDOM for it shall be built upon a solid foundation - So be it everlasting -- Mine word I have given unto thee and no man shall void MINE WORD -- So be it and Selah -- For I say unto thee MINE WORD shall not pass away - for this is THE NEW DAY - THE NEW DISPENSATION I give unto thee -- Ye are no longer under the old law - for the old shall pass as obsolete - and it shall not bind thee - for I say that the old law is not for Mine people THIS DAY - for I bring unto thee a new commandment "This Day" I say: "Come ye out from amongst them which have put their foot against me -- Come ye forth and I shall anoint thee with the water of Everlasting Life"- and nothing shall touch thee which is of darkness -

neither shall ye walk the way of <u>flesh</u> - for it shall be mine way - the way of Spirit -- And this I have spoken for the good of all -- So be it and Selah -- Let them who will hear - fear not for them which set foot against <u>me</u> for I am responsible for mine own self -- Pray that they awaken - and be ye alert unto the cunning of men - for I say his cunning shall trip him up ---

Bear ye witness of mine words - and be ye blest of me and by me.

Recorded by Sister Thedra

Sori Sori -- For this day let it be said that one shall come unto thee for to give unto thee a portion which shall be given unto them which await it -- So be it and Selah -- Ye shall stand alert and prepared to receive him and that which he has for thee -- So be it and Selah

The House of the Lord Shall Stand

Sori Sori -- Be ye as one prepared to receive this one which I bring unto thee - for there is but one which is prepared to receive him – and he hast waited long that he might speak unto thee -- The time is now come when he might speak unto thee - yet it shall be for the good of all men, - all mankind - for all shall profit thereby---

Now let it be understood that he hast come thru the Great and Mighty Council - for the purpose of lifting up mankind -- So let it be according to the Father's will ---

Ye shall now record that which he says - for the good of all which are to follow thee -- So be it there shall be few which shall reject his words - yet they are the weak of spirit - and know not that which they say -- Blest are they which receive him - for he comes in the name of the Father - and I am with him that this might serve them well -- So let it be -- Amen ---

For this day I greet thee O my beloved Sister - as one long away - long awaited -- I say unto thee - thou hast gone out from us -- While we have awaited thy coming - thou hast wandered in darkness - wherein thou hast labored and waited - wherein thou hast suffered and cried out for deliverance -- Too - thou hast asked that they be delivered alike -- Therein is thy own salvation - for it is given unto thee to see their plight and have compassion upon them -- Yet thou hast not put thy foot upon their neck - neither hast thou put thy hand into their pocket ---

Now ye shall give unto them that which I give unto thee thee - and it shall be mine word - and it shall not be for <u>them</u> to judge me - neither mine words -- While I am responsible for mine word - they are responsible for their acceptance or rejection -- I say - pity are they which sit in judgment of me and mine word -- While I say pity are they, I too say: Sad are they which set foot against thee - or against "The House of The Lord"---

Wast it not said: that "The House of The Lord shall stand" - it is so! For I am one which shall guard and keep safe the door -- I am one which shall keep the way of righteousness open unto them which seek righteousness -- Them which enter into the gate shall find peace therein, for it shall be established within them-- Blest shall they be ---

Behold in me the Light which I Am - I am come of the Light - I am within the Light - for I Am the Light -- I am he which is ONE in the Light - ONE of The Light - and of the ONE I AM - thus I speak unto thee - for I AM ONE with the ALL ---

Thou hast given of thyself that <u>they</u> be blest - thou hast given of thyself that there be Light - and it shall be recorded in the records - kept for all eternity - and none shall say thee naught - none shall stay thee - none shall take from thee one iota of thy inheritance -- None shall deny thee thy reward - for it is said: All shall be given unto thee that thou hast earned - and rightfully so. So be it that thy inheritance is assured thee - I say thy full inheritance is thine - so be it by Divine decree -- So shall it be as the Father hast willed it ---

By the Divine Council and the Mighty Host - I am given the authority - the power and authority to speak thusly - and rightfully so - for the time is propitious and the hour now strikes when ye shall speak out - that all might hear - that all be blest -- It is said - thy tongue shall be loosed and ye shall proclaim the WORD - and it shall be manifest with them which believeth in the Light which is manifested in me -- So be it that I shall touch thee and they shall know that thou hast been touched - for I say unto thee: Thou shall speak the word and it shall be made manifest before thy eyes -- So be it and Selah ---

Be ye as one prepared for that which I shall give unto thee to do -- So be it I shall bless thee - and ye shall bless them as thou hast been blest -- Let them prepare themself as thou hast prepared thyself -- Let them BE the sacrificial lamb - let them be the crucified -- Let them be the portion which they prepare for their fellows - let them drink the cup they prepare for another -- Let them come as little ones - and bring unto thee their gifts - their poor broken pieces which they have gathered up the fragments from their own table ---

Let them come bringing the fragments - and lay them at thy feet - and ye shall bless them and make of them new - and they shall remember no more their foolishness - their rigamaroles and foolish sayings ---

They shall put from them all selfishness - greed - hatred - fornication and blasphemy -- They shall be unto thee servant and brother - they shall be as thy hand and thy foot - giving of themself that all be blest -- So be it and Selah ---

I say - ye shall bear witness of mine word - for I know that which I say -- So shall it be -- And for this do I say - record ye mine words - that they too bear witness of mine words ---

Be ye blest this day --

I am

Recorded by Sister Thedra

Each unto His Part

Sori Sori -- For this day let it be said that there shall be one which shall come unto thee - and he shall give unto thee a part - and he shall bless thee - and he shall be as one which hast been prepared for his part which he shall have with thee -- So be it and Selah---

Hear ye me and I shall tell thee of a plan which hast been formulated within the <u>Great</u> and <u>Mighty</u> <u>Council</u> - and therein is the fortune of mine plan ---

Bear ye in mind that I am not alone in this - for there are many which are mine assistants and Brothers -- We come at this time that all men be lifted up - yet all men know not the way of everlasting life ---

They seek dark places and the way of destruction - yet - I speak unto thee that they too might find their way -- Let it be for the ones which seek that ye labor - for the weak shall fall by the way - and they shall cry on out for help ---

These shall come seeking - inquiring - and these shall be given that which they are prepared to receive - these shall be blest for they shall receive in proportion to their capacity -- So be it that they shall be as ones alert - and willing to learn -- Fear - not that ye fail them - for <u>they</u> shall put their foot forward - <u>they</u> shall put out their hand to do their part - and <u>then</u> - ye shall give unto them of thy strength - energy and wisdom - for hast thou not made the way clear for them - hast thou not gone the long way to bless them - for this art thou prepared to assist <u>them</u>!

Let it prove profitable unto thee - for it shall be thy victory - and thy own part shall be as thy reward - for it is kept for thee -- And it shall profit them which seek - to be as ones fortuned to partake of thy own fortune - for it shall bless all which are so prepared -- So be it and Selah.

Recorded by Sister Thedra

The Earth's Pathway

Sori Sori -- For this day let it be said: There is but one God - the Father and He has the power and authority to bring thee out of bondage - yet it is by thine own will that ye are delivered ---

Therefore I say unto thee: Be ye as one blest to be as one delivered for it is now come when ye shall walk as one unbound - as one free from the gravitation - and free from the attraction of the moon -- And at no time shall ye fail - for it is so ordered that ye be brot out of bondage -

The Earth now passes her initiation into the pathway which hast been cleared for her - and she shall endure - and no man shall say me nay! for it is for this that we of the Mighty Host hast stood by as ones prepared to lift her up - to bring her into her new place wherein she shall be made new ---

The hour strikes when the Earth and her children shall be no more bound in darkness -- I say the dawn is come - yet unto thee I say: Ye see not the Light - for it is as tho ye were looking thru a dark glass -- While the darkness shall pass and ye shall see clearly within the allotted time - I say there is a season of laughter and of weeping - a season of sowing and reaping - a season of gladness - a season of joy and sadness a season of portions - a season of notions - a season of water - a season of drought - a season of knowing - a season of doubt ---

Now ye shall go forth as a sower goes forth to his labor -- Ye shall be as one prepared - for the season is upon thee when many seed shall fall upon prepared soil - and they shall be nursed - nourished and they shall come into maturity - and they shall find their mark - they shall do that which was intended from the beginning -- Thus it is that I say: Be ye as one prepared for a greater part -- So be it I shall speak again and again - and ye shall hear me -- So be it and Selah---

Recorded by Sister Thedra

Lift Up Thine Eyes

Sori Sori -- Mighty is the power and wisdom of the God of Heaven and Earth - for He is sent of the Father - the CAUSE of thy being -- Let it be understood that we come in the name of the Father which hast given unto us being - therefore I say unto thee - we are not of the nether world neither are we underlings of any false god which has set himself up -- For we have waited and watched for this day - and we have kept the way unto the Father's House - preparing the way that all be brot back in due season -- And it behooves me to say unto thee - the time is now come when ye shall see the Glory of the Lord - for he shall be unto thee that which the Father would have him be -- He hast revealed his presence unto to thee - and thou hast found him the Founder of the Temple wherein Peace abides -- Let it be said that peace shall abide in the House of the Lord - and none shall tear down or destroy the house which is built upon a solid foundation -- I say - build ye well - and stand ye firm and no man shall cast thee out ---

I have set up the banner of righteousness upon thy native soil - and I have planted the staff deeply - and no man - no people shall uproot it. Yet the fog hast obscured the banner - it flieth high - and man hast hung low his head - therefore he hast failed to see the banner which flieth above his head ---

Let him raise his sight - let him lift his eyes and see that which is above him -- He looks and sees not - he cries and hears no answer - yet I say it is well that he lifts his eyes unto the hills from which cometh his help---

The law is clear: As one is prepared so does he receive - as a man prepareth himself so does he become ---

Therefore I say unto man: Lift up thine eyes and behold the Glory of the Lord - for He is with thee and He stands above thee with His hand lifted in praise of the Great One which is the ALL - the ONE - the CREATOR of all that is desirable and eternal -- The LAW is exact and it faileth not - therefore I say - be ye as one mindful of thy SOURCE OF BEING - for HE and He alone is the Father - Solen Aum Solen - which holds thee within His bosom and which hast provided for thee - He hast sent Sons and Daughters unto thee that the way be made clear for thee - that ye may return unto Him unscathed - unharmed ---

Blest are they which do return -- So be it and Selah --

Recorded by Sister Thedra

They Shall Apply Wisdom unto Their Knowledge

Sori Sori -- Let this day be the first of a new age - a New Day - and give unto me credit for knowing that which I say - for I know --

I say this is the "First day of a new Age" wherein ye shall come to know many things which have been hidden from thee - for it is now come when great revelation shall be given unto thee -- There are many which walk with thee that this might be accomplished ---

I say - the day shall bring forth such revelation as hast not been given in time past - for the people of Earth hast not begun to arouse themself - and to enquire for themself the meaning of the 'Signs of the Times' - and they have begun to cry out for light -- No longer do they sit and cry - they are now astir and restless - they are prone to forgetfulness - yet there are ones which shall remember - and these shall be the doers - and accomplish that which is given unto them to do -- These shall be as ones prepared for greater things ---

Now it is written that they shall seek knowledge and apply wisdom unto their knowledge - they shall turn from their own way and seek the way of truth - and they shall be the ones which turn from war and destruction - they shall lift up their fellow man and be unto him a comfort - and bless him as the brother -- They shall be as the older brother unto the weaker - and they shall know that he is the brother - of one Father created! So be it that they shall be prepared for the <u>greater part</u> -- Not in any place shall they find peace on one hand and war on the other - for they shall be no part of war - I say war shall be no more. They shall put from them all hatred - all false gods - all anger and maliciousness - all hypocrisy -- They shall be as ones which love righteousness <u>for</u> <u>righteousness</u> <u>sake</u> -- They shall be as ones which have the key unto the door of knowledge - and they shall turn it by their own hand - each in his own way - and according to the LAW ---

No man shall be unto his brother a yoke - neither shall he give unto him more than he can bear ---

It is written that babes shall not eat of the harder substance - yet he shall be so prepared - for in due season his teeth shall be sufficient unto his growth and needs - for this has been provided unto him from the beginning ---

Waste not thy energy on the one which hast not the will to learn - neither condemn ye him - for he shall be as one provided for - and he shall not be overlooked - for he too is numbered and accounted for - there is a place provided him wherein he might grow and prosper in spirit ---

I say the lowly and the poor in spirit shall be as the ones which shall be the wards of the wise and prudent - and they shall be as ones prepared in the school wherein they shall be put - and they shall be as the wards of the <u>wise</u> - for it is so ordained -- So be it and Selah ---

Recorded by Sister Thedra

Spirit Cleaneth

Sori Sori -- Be ye as one responsible for this which shall be given unto thee for them which seek the Light -- Let it be profitable unto them which seek - and seek they shall ---

While it is not yet revealed unto them - that which is revealed unto thee - they shall seek that they too - might know -- They shall seek and find - they shall ask for light (revelation/ truth/ understanding) - they shall find it profitable unto them -- While it is given me to be one appointed unto them that seek - I am now come that they might know that which shall be of great benefit unto them -- Mine is a part - and separate from the way of flesh - mine is the way of Spirit -- Let them which seek the Way of <u>Truth</u> and <u>Life</u> seek within the Spirit - for it is the Life -- Wherein is it said that 'flesh shall perish'- so it does and shall. While spirit shall not perish- spirit shall remain spirit in its purity ---

Flesh is contaminated by man - and the spirit purifieth - for as the water washes clean the garment - so does the spirit cleaneth the fortunes of man - it transmutes and maketh clean -- Wherein is it said - that the flesh is animated by Spirit?

Many there be which claim the flesh to be pure - yet I say unto thee: flesh is flesh! And it entereth not into the realm of Light as flesh -- There are ones which teach that flesh entereth into the "heavens" - yet I say it goeth not past the world of illusion - the dream state---

Yet the "heavens" are the worlds beyond the imagination of man - and are the real - while the flesh is partially of the real - for the spirit <u>animates</u> that which is flesh ---

While the flesh is the unknowing the spirit is the knower and the doer -- Therefore it behooves man to know that which SPIRIT sayeth - that which Spirit doeth ---

Let it be known that I am the / one of spirit which is sent at this time that this might be said - that they might discern truth from illusion/ false - for many false doctrines are taught to the unknowing ones - for this I say - pity are they which betray themself or their trust -- There be ones which set themself up as wise and holy - knowing not they are in darkness -- While it is said - "Seek ye the Light"- they think themself prepared to enter into the Holy of Holies - wherein they may not enter before they are prepared ---

They praise themself and sing praise unto their unknown god - and they bind themself with their own opinions and false teaching -- pity are they for they know not that which they do - it is given unto me to come that they might know ---

I say - there are none so foolish as the one which <u>thinks</u> himself wise - he shall be brot face to face with his foolishness -- Bless thyself by seeking the Light - and one shall come to lead thee -- O man! O man of Earth - lift up thine eyes and see the Light - let thine feet be swift to serve the Light - swift to do the Father's <u>Will</u> - for thine own is not of great profit unto thee - it hast led thee far afield -- Why - O why - hast thou slept so long? Awaken! and come forth as a Son of the Most High! So let it profit thee - for this hast He sent me ---

Recorded by Sister Thedra

The Law

Sori Sori -- Wherein is it said that there shall be great things accomplished this day - it shall be -- And not any man shall put aside the law or nullify it - for it is now come when man shall come to know he is under the law - he shall thereby abide - and he shall be delivered out by such law ---

He shall be as one with the law - and he shall not transgress the law. For this hast he been commanded to obey the law - that he might be free of it - for within the law he is free - and because of the law -- Let him understand THE LAW which brings him forth - and wherein he shall find his freedom ---

When he hast complied with the law - he shall find it just and compensating - he shall be as one free - and he shall know freedom as he hast not known ---

Now it is said - the law shall not bind him - for he shall be one in harmony with it - he shall rejoice - for it shall be his freedom -- And no man shall set himself over the law for he too comes under it - while he knows not the greater law -- Yet for this do we of the Mighty Council bring unto thee the higher law - that the lower might be brot unto the attention of all men - that they be made one with the higher -- Now it shall be understood that there is nothing higher than the LAW of which we speak - for this let it be said we are one with it -- We move and have our being as one - one with the law - one within the law - for <u>all</u> <u>things</u> move and exist according to a law -- Behold - I say unto thee - Behold the law - - see the working thereof ---

Bless thyself to see - and to know --

See and Know --

Recorded by Sister Thedra

Mission Statement

Give the truth to the world. Let it be received where it will. Many will read the messages. Some will accept the truth, others will read through curiosity, a few will ridicule. Yet to all is the truth given, and to all remains the power of choice.

The hope of the world in these times is in spiritualizing all forms of activity---promoting understanding through love and service. These must be the watchwords if the world is to come into lasting peace. We are trying to influence a world that is going astray and could cause undreamed of suffering. We are trying to overcome the thought of materialists and to bring a spiritual outlook into the earthly life. We need the help of all on earth who can think in spiritual terms. The great battle to be fought now is between the spiritual and the material, between idealism and carnalism. You can help by spreading the word---we are asking that you help because the battle may be long and the victory far away.

Halls of Light is not allied with any sect, denomination, political entity, organization, neither endorses nor opposes any cause. There are no dues for membership. Halls of Light is self-supporting through its own voluntary contributions. Halls of Light has but one purpose: to help through encouragement and understanding...

To contact the publishers or to obtain copies of our other books, please contact us at:

Email: goldtown11@gmail.com

Web: https://www.whoamiandwhyamihere.com/order-online

Sananda's Appearance

Be ye as one which hast heard Mine Voice and responded unto it - for I speak that ye hear, and I say that which is wise and prudent.

Let it be known that 1, the Lord thy God hast spoken and bear ye witness of Me, for I have made manifest Mineself that ye might know Me - and for this wast these manifestations made.

I say that I have made Mineself manifest that ye might see Me with thine mortal eyes; that ye might bear witness of Me. Yet thine companions saw and believed not; neither did they hear, for they were selfish and unprepared - yet, did I deny them?

I say; I came that they which would might see and hear. I went and came again unto Mine own. So be it that I have found; I have given unto the found that they which know not might know; that they might come to know as thou knowest.

Yet, how many hast turned from Me and persecuted thee for Mine Word. It is said, "Woe unto them which persecute Mine servants." is it not the law which they set into motion?

Yea Mine beloved, I say they bring about their own downfall. So be it that I am a compassionate one, and I would that they know what they do. So be it they shall learn well their lessons. So let it be, for this is the mercy of God, the One which hast sent Me.

So be it. I AM The Wayshower, the Lord thy God

I AM Sananda

About the Late Sister Thedra

Since the later part of the last Century, the Kumara wisdom has begun to reemerge into the world. This process began with the late Sister Thedra, whom Jesus Christ appeared physically to while on her deathbed and spontaneously healed her of cancer while she was in the Yucatan, where she had gone to accept her fate and the will of our Lord Jesus Christ.

That is when something miraculous occurred. Jesus spoke to her saying, "My name is Esu Sananda Kumara" and then sent Thedra down to the Monastery of the Seven Rays in Peru to learn the Kumara wisdom. After five years, Thedra was told to return to the United States where she founded the Association of Sananda and Sanat Kumara at Mt. Shasta in California.

While heading this organization, Thedra channeled many messages from Sananda and taught the Kumara wisdom. He introduced himself to her by his true name, "Sananda Kumara" And it was by his command that Sister Thedra went to Peru but eventually left upon being told that her experience there was complete. She then traveled to Mt. Shasta in California and founded the Association of Sananda and Sanat Kumara. A.S.S.K.

You ask, Is There a difference between Jesus and Sananda? Our Lord's name given at birth by his Father Joseph and his beloved mother Mary was Yeshua, thus being of the house of David and the order of Yoseph, he would be called Yeshua ben Yoseph. The Roman Emperors placed the name of Jesus upon the sir name of Yeshua after the Emperor Justinian adopted Christianity as the official faith of Rome and ordered that the sacred books be compiled upon approval of a specially appointed counsel appointed by the Emperor into a recognizable and uniform work titled "The Bible". Prior to this, there never was a Bible per se.

There existed until the time of the Emperor's edict, a selection of many Sacred texts that were employed in the Sacred Teachings, many of which were copies of what the Greeks had transposed from the original texts in the Libraries of Alexandria which were originally compiled by Alexander the Great, and were destroyed by Julius Caesar, fearing that they might prove dangerous to the rule of a Caesar, an Earthly God.

In addition, it was to keep the knowledge of Alexander's Libraries out of the hands of the Ptolemy's who were said to be descended from his bloodline. At the time, Caesar had no way of knowing that vast portions of the Library were already in the Americas, in the Great Universities of the Inca, and in possession of the Mayans.

Yeshua spent many years in the East after his ascension. The Good Sheppard, upon his appearances to the Apostles after his ascension, told them that he was going to tend to his Father's other sheep; which meant, plainly, that he was continuing upon his sacred journey. As The Ascended One, Yeshua took to himself the name of Sananda, meaning the Christed One, and Sananda was thus embraced forevermore by the Great Solar Brotherhood. To many of you this is all new, to others it will be received as a welcome easing of the wall that has so long separated two sides of the same coin. This is being placed into the ethers and the matrix of thought at this time, as it is the time of The Great Awakening, and the Christos is already emerging into the new consciousness.

Authority to use the name of Sananda was given to Sister Thedra when Jesus, (Sananda), appeared to her in the Yucatan and cured her instantly of the cancer that had taken over her body. Further, he allowed a picture of his countenance to be taken at that time that she might realize the occurrence was more than a dream. Thedra had a large format camera called a 620 that she used to take the picture of Sananda.

Sanada's Message to her by Sister Thedra: "Sori Sori: Mine hand I have placed upon thine head, and I have given unto thee the authority to use Mine name. Give unto them the name Sananda, by which they shall know Me as the Lord thy God - the Son of God, sent that ye be made to know me, the One sent from out The Inner Temple that there be Light in the world of men. Now it is come when ones which have the will to follow Me shall come to know Me by that name which I commanded thee to give unto the world as Mine New name.

There are many that shall call upon the name of Jesus, yet they will deny the new name as they are want to do. Unto thee I give assurance that I am the One sent that there be Light in the world of men. Now let this be understood, that they that deny Mine New Name deny Me by any name. So be it I have appointed thee Mine spokesman; I've given unto thee the power and authority to speak for being that which I AM. And I say unto thee Mine child whom I have called forth and anointed thee with the Holy Spirit, thy name shall be as it is now called, Thedra, that name I spoke unto thee from out the ethers, and thou heard Me and accepted that which I gave unto thee; and wherein have I deceived thee? Wherein have I forgotten thee, or left thee alone?"

I say unto thee: "Mine hand is upon thee and I shall sustain thee and you shall come to know that which I have kept for thee. So be it that I have kept thy reward, and at no time shall it be dissipated or scattered, for it is intact. So let this Mine Word suffice them which question thee - let them question, and I shall bear witness for thee. For do I not know Mine servants from the traitors? Do I not reward Mine servants according unto their works or merits? I speak that they might know that I am mindful of Mine servants, that I am not a poor puny priest who has forgotten his servants.

"I say unto them: Mine servants shall be glorified above the crowned heads of the nations which have set themselves apart, and denied Me Mine part of Mine word for they have turned from Me in their conceit and forgetfulness. Now let this go on record as Mine Word, and I shall give unto them proof, which are of a mind to follow Me.

So be it as I have spoken and I am not finished; I shall speak again and again, and I shall rise Mine Voice against them which set foot against Mine servants, and they shall be as ones cast out. So let them ask of Me and I shall enlighten them. So be it I know whereof I speak. Be ye as ones blest to accept Me and know Me for that which I AM." On Saturday, June 13, 1992, at exactly 10.00 PM, at the age of 92, Sister Thedra made her final transition from the comfort of her own bed. When the time arrived, she simply took one small breath and slipped quietly away, without pomp or fanfare.

She left as she had lived: as a humble servant for the greater good. The messages included were given to Sister Thedra shortly before her transition. They are compiled here to give you some idea of the significance of her passing and of the expansion of the work, as she is now free of the physical limitations and the pain of the past. Her work now in the higher realms will simply be an extension of that work.

Divine Explanations

Part - I

The following explanations and definitions of terms used by Sananda (Jesus) and the various Sibors were given by Sananda through direct revelation. They are not alphabetical. These explanations should be read over and over.

- - - - - - - - - - -

"My Beloved Sibors please give us plainly the definitions of the following words that there may be no error on our part." - Thedra.

THEMSELF? What is the explanation of your terminology of "Themself" – "themselves"?

"I (Sananda) say unto thee mine beloved, they which would be unto thee a vessel, unto thee a sibor, unto thee teacher, are as ones enlightened of the Father, enlightened of the Father for the light is in them.

They know their parts well, they have their memory, they have mastered the elements, they can do all the things which I do and they take unto "themself" no credit for they have overcome self. They are self-less. Now I say unto them: them which work with thee are the Selfless ones. They ask <u>nothing</u> for "themself." Now while this is true they are as one.

They are within the great brotherhood of the Selfless Ones - the Ones clothed in white. They are as the Royal Assembly - and each unto his own, yet each for all and all for one. Now while in thy world, they (of thy world) are <u>selfish</u> and they are not for the whole - they ask for self and I speak of these as the selfish ones. I speak unto them in terms which they shall come to know and therein is wisdom.

I say that they shall be responsible for "themself" and as a world of me I say they shall be responsible for their society; they "themself" have created it. Now I speak unto thee mine beloved, I say "ye shall be responsible for thyself. He shall be responsible for himself. They as a whole shall be responsible for that which they have created, while thou art responsible unto thyself for thine part - and not held accountable for theirs. Be it so."

BELEIS? "Mighty is the word and great the power thereof. I say unto thee this word carries with it the part of surrender. The word is the release of power - that which is sent forth by the one which asks of the Father His blessing. It is the surrender of the self - the complete surrender of the personal will and letting the Father's will be accomplished in all things through thee. "<u>So</u> <u>be</u> <u>it</u>" - it the accomplishment, the acceptance of the Father's plan."

SELAH? - "The word carries the Seal of Truth - meaning it is without error - no mistake - it is the verification of Truth - not subject to change.

SIBET? – "The Sibet is one which has offered or presented himself as a candidate for the greater learning and for the greater initiation. He comes as an empty vessel that he may be filled. So be it."

SIBOR? - "I am the Sibor of Sibors." - "The Sibor is one which has been illumined of God the Father. He has returned unto the Father purified. He has gone the Royal Road - which means he has overcome death. He has mastered the lower elements - he controls the elements. He can raise the dead - heal the sick - he can create like unto the Father for he has finished his course and won the victory and returned unto the Father the Victor. So be it."

"I am the Sibor of Sibors. I am the first born of Him which hast sent me. Sananda."

LEGIRONS? - "Beloved - I say unto thee: thy opinions and thy dogmas are not the least of these - neither thy creeds. Be it ever that these are great and heavy ones. Now let it be understood that a leg-iron is something which holds thee bound. It is something which holds thee, it keeps thee fast, wherein progress is not possible. Now that progress be made possible, ye shall cut away the legirons.

Knowest thou these bound by legirons? These are to be pitied, they drag them with them, impeding their progress - and they are as ones bound! They are not free - are they? While they serve their sentence - they are as ones bound - they are bond-men - they are bound men - men bound. Now let me say I too am a "bondsman." I came that they may be free. I say I bring unto thee the law which thou shall obey - unto the letter - then I shall give unto thee that which I have kept for thee. Be ye as one prepared for that.

PREPARATION? Now - preparation - what do you mean by "preparation?" "This my beloved is the part which they shall do - the part of preparation is: cleaning thyself of all the opinions, indoctrinations of man. The cup must be emptied. This is thy part, the becoming the "'little child" unopinionated, unscathed and unmarred with or by their doctrines, creeds and crafts. I say the child is unindoctrinated and un-opinonated and is the virgin mind – (yet it does not remain so long in this world). While the little child represents the empty cup - the empty vessel, the Virgin Spirit, it is given unto the child to be one which has come from other realms and to have been in many embodiments, many times: yet the symbol of virginity. Wherein is it said there are none innocent among thee?

WHEREIN I AM? - "Now while thou art yet within the world of men - I am within mine Father's realm, the place wherein there is no darkness, wherein <u>ALL</u> things are known. I say wherein <u>ALL</u> things are known, wherein there is <u>No</u> mystery.

And too - I say when thou hast attained unto thy Royal Road, when thou hast become part of the Royal Assembly, thou shall know as I - thou shall be as I - thou shall be brought into the place wherein I am, for I say unto thee this is attainment. This is the day of Attainment, the day of "becoming," the day of thy salvation. Know ye that this is Mine day - the day for which thou hast waited? I say unto thee: "This is the day of fulfillment. This is Mine Day. Mine Day is come ---"

What is meant by "ALL THE LANDS OF THE EARTH?"- "This I mean, all the lands of the Earth. I have said it, I mean it as I have said it and there is no mystery of or to it."

ALL MANKIND? "This is Mine people - Mine children - Mine flock - Mine Church - Mine brethren - Mine congregation unto whom I shall minister. By Mine own hand shall they be fed and led. These have I came to find. Are not all <u>hu</u>-man beings considered "Man kind"? by thine own standards. Yet all men are not of me."

WHAT DO YOU MEAN - "WILL IT SO"? - "There is power in the "WILL" and the power which they use to create their own torment and confusion is misused energy. Yet they will this - they will it so. Now when ye will to serve me ye give unto me thy undivided attention, the whole heart - thy heart - thine ALL. Yet I say that they which doth attempt to serve me with one hand and the dragon with the other has not willed to serve me. They are not of me - they are not of Mine flock. I say they are either with me or against me. I cannot accept the one hand while they reserve the other for the dragon. They are not wholeheartedly mine.

I make no compromises with the dragon. Mine shall come out from them and surrender unto me themself - their all - without reservation. This is willing it so - for they will the Father's will be done in them, through them, by them. They leave no energy that the dragon may use. They use all their energy to serve me. This is mine word unto thee."

WHAT IS DARKNESS? - "Thine Un-Knowing - thy darkness comes from the fall of man - which one was with God the Father perfect which didst have his memory blanked from him when he didst transgress."

MAYAS VEIL? - "The result of such unknowing - the darkness which man has brought upon himself. The part he has created for himself."

WHAT DOES IT MEAN TO <u>BETRAY</u> <u>ONES</u> <u>SELF</u>? - "This is the sad part for first the 'fall' came from his betrayal - and it hast resulted in the fall - in the veil of Maya - the "illusion" and in thy un-knowing - in thy own darkness."

WHAT OF BETRAYING "HIS OWN TRUST"? - "The plan is all inclusive and includes <u>all</u> - yet there are ones unaware of the "plan" - (and they are not as included in this temple as yet) - no personal reference unto the ones within this temple. Now when one becomes aware of his part, he is given the law and it is provided for his own good and he has the law clearly stated, plainly recorded, and he turns his face away - that he may hide from it. He puts his fingers into his ears that he may not hear it. He gives unto his benefactors the bitter cup and he goes his own willful way.

He has betrayed himself for he shall be caught up short of his course. When he has been given a chance - a "part" within the plan and he has committed himself, he has the responsibility given unto him for that "part" and should he be so foolish as to betray his trust he shall be like unto one which has thrown overboard his <u>own</u> life belt - poor foolish ones!"

WISDOM? - What is meant by the word "Wisdom?" - "Wisdom is that which is light, the knowledge of the law and its proper use. The right use of the law - and this Mine children is Mine part. I come that ye may BECOME wise! Wisdom is thy divine gift - not of man, for man of Earth is foolish indeed - and he is nothing save that which the Father has endowed him. All else is of the world of "illusion" which shall pass into nothingness in the Light which I Am."

WHAT IS THE "PEARL OF GREAT PRICE, THE PRICELESS PEARL? - "That which I offer thee - thy freedom, thy salvation from bondage - thine inheritance in full - Mine word which is not purchased with coin - not bought, neither is it sold. It is the wisdom of which I speak. Mine offer unto thee is without price - it is the 'pearl' - "Mine Pearl."

WHY ARE MIS-SPELLED AND GRAMMATICAL ERRORS USED IN THESE SCRIPTS? - "I am not a conformist. I am not concerned with the letters of man for I am He which has come that they be unbound by their fetters. I say unto them which desireth the letter - unto them the letter.

I say unto thee: be ye as ones free from such bondage. I stand ready to free thee from thy bondage. Unto thee I say - give unto the letter no thought. <u>Hear</u> what I <u>say</u> for I shall say it in many ways as becomes me and serves mine purpose. I say I am no stranger in thine midst. While they know me not, I know them. I see them bowing down before the Golden Calf - and they worship at the shrines which they have set up. (Their own standards of education.) They guild them and bring unto them burnt offerings - yet they close me out.

Be ye not so foolish. <u>Be</u> <u>ye</u> <u>not</u> <u>so</u> <u>foolish</u>! I am come that ye might have Light - Wisdom - Freedom which is the Father's will. While the letter changeth and passeth away - and the letter is not the law - the letter is of no consequence other than to cause thee to see the "Word." The word is the power which shall provoke thine mind into action and thy mind shall be free from the letter. See what is meant within the Word, and let thine mind be staid on <u>me</u> - the Light, the Way - Truth and Wisdom."

"I am He which hast come - that ye be free: forever free. I am Sananda - Son of God. Once known as the Nazarine, He which was born of Mary, Ward of Joseph.

Recorded by Thedra

Part - 2

THE WHITE BROTHERHOOD AND THE EMERALD CROSS.

THE MANY QUESTIONS ABOUT THE WHITE BROTHERHOOD AND THE ORDER OF THE EMERALD CROSS MAY BE EXPLAINED IN A FEW SIMPLE WORDS.

ONE HAS TO EARN THE RIGHT TO BECOME A MEMBER - EITHER IN THIS LIFE OR OTHERS BEFORE OR AFTER - NONE ENTER UNPREPARED.

THE WHITE BROTHERHOOD - or - THE ROYAL ASSEMBLY is of the Realms of Light---not of Earth. The Ascended Masters have proven themself in the school of Earth (THE SCHOOL FOR GODS) who have trodden the path of INITIATION - overcome the trials and temptations of the mundane world - who have gained their freedom and ascended as the Lord Jesus Christ (Sananda). They have gone the ROYAL ROAD.

Knowing the path of the Initiate -- and its pitfalls -- and sorrow, they extend a hand in Fellowship - LOVE and WISDOM - NEVER depriving the candidate an opportunity to learn his lessons well -- for this is His salvation -- for this do they proffer their hand, NOT to do our part for us, but rather that we become strong and free by our own strength.

The Royal Assembly or the White Brotherhood have known all of the heartaches, the longing, crucifications, temptations and JOYS of the aspirant -- the candidate -- the Master -- the Sibor -- herein lies their strength, their understanding, their great love for us on the path.

INITIATION - Thy preparation for the inner temple. Each step is an initiation. One step at a time - the overcoming of self - the world - the becoming that which I am.

COSMOS - That which is unseen throughout many universes by thy eyes. Great is the expanse of the Father's Kingdom and the total thereof is referred to as "throughout the Cosmos."

LORD'S STRANGE ACT - This I shall reveal in Mine own time.

WALK WHICH WAY THY CROWN TILTS NOT - as a Son of God. Do honor unto thy Father Mother God - and thou shall be as one which has the Royal Raiment upon thine shoulders - and ye shall wear it in honor and with dignity.

WHEN IT SAYS IT IS RECORDED - WHEREIN IS IT RECORDED? - In the secret place - in the eth - and within the inner temple - and wherein thou art are many things recorded - which I do speak of. Ye shall see these recordings when thou doth enter into the secret place of Mine abode. I say ye shall read the records wherein are written the records of all thy travels from the time ye left the Father Mother God until thine return unto him.

WHAT IS MICHAEL'S FLAMING SWORD? - "The "Sword of Truth and justice."

Recorded by Sister Thedra

Other Books by TNT Publishing

Who am I and Why Am I here?

The Significance of Existence

Death and the Incredible Life After

Fear of Death Removed

Paradise Regained

Spiritual Laws Revealed

Unseen Forces

Too Good to Be True

The Truth of Life in the Spirit World

He Who Has Ears

The Great Awakening, Volumes I thru VII

The Great Awakening, Volume VIII,
THE WHITE STAR OF THE EAST

The Great Awakening, Volume IX,
I THE LORD GOD SAY UNTO THEM

The Great Awakening, Volume X,
MINE INTERCOM MESSAGES FROM THE REALMS OF LIGHT

The Great Awakening, Volume XI,
THE BOOK OF THE LORD

The Great Awakening, Volume XII thru XV,
TEMPLE TEACHINGS FROM THE HIGHER REALMS

Transfiguration Volumes I thru Volume VIII

Contact us at

Email: goldtown11@gmail.com

Web: https://www.whoamiandwhyamihere.com/order-online

www.ingramcontent.com/pod-product-compliance
Lightning Source LLC
LaVergne TN
LVHW051550070426
835507LV00021B/2498